Refuse

CanLit in Ruins

edited by
HANNAH McGREGOR, JULIE RAK, and **ERIN WUNKER**

Book*hug
TORONTO

FIRST EDITION

Individual texts copyright © 2018 by the authors
Introductions copyright © 2018 by Hannah McGregor, Julie Rak and Erin Wunker

The production of this book was made possible through the generous assistance of the Canada Council for the Arts and the Ontario Arts Council. Book*hug also acknowledges the support of the Government of Canada through the Canada Book Fund and the Government of Ontario through the Ontario Book Publishing Tax Credit and the Ontario Book Fund.

Book*hug acknowledges the land on which it operates. For thousands of years it has been the traditional land of the Huron-Wendat, the Seneca, and most recently, the Mississaugas of the Credit River. Today, this meeting place is still the home to many Indigenous people from across Turtle Island, and we are grateful to have the opportunity to work on this land.

Library and Archives Canada Cataloguing in Publication

Refuse : CanLit in ruins / Erin Wunker, Julie Rak, Hannah McGregor, editors. —First edition.

Issued in print and electronic formats.
ISBN 978-1-77166-431-8 (softcover)
ISBN 978-1-77166-432-5 (HTML)
ISBN 978-1-77166-433-2 (PDF)
ISBN 978-1-77166-434-9 (Kindle)

1. Canadian literature (English) —History and criticism. 2. Race discrimination in literature. 3. Imperialism in literature. 4. Social classes in literature. 5. Sex discrimination in literature. 6. Literature and society—Canada—History. I. Wunker, Erin, 1979–, editor II. Rak, Julie, 1966–, editor III. McGregor, Hannah, editor

PS8071.R44 2018   C810.9   C2018-904944-8
C2018-904945-6

Printed in Canada

for all the complainants

'A complaint: when a collective is necessary to bring something about.'
—Sara Ahmed

Contents

Introduction
Living in the Ruins

HANNAH McGREGOR, JULIE RAK, ERIN WUNKER

"A lot of sad feelings about CanLit. A lot of sad feelings about just fuckin' being alive."

—Katherena Vermette, *Can't Lit*[1]

We think of "refuse" in many ways. It is saying "no" to the serious inequities, prejudices, and hierarchies that exist within Canadian literature as an industry (often shortened to "CanLit") and an area of academic study. "Refuse" is another word for garbage, for waste. And what wastes our time, and our lives as writers and teachers, is the kind of endorsement of the status quo that we want to see taken out of CanLit. But "refuse" can also mean "re/fuse," to put together what has been torn apart, evoking the idea that, after something is destroyed, something better can take its place. No matter what we mean by "refuse," this much is clear: after a series of controversies and scandals, the signifier "CanLit" currently lies in ruins.

Something's rotten in the (nation-)state of CanLit. And to point to that rot, we first have to do a few things. We have to name the symptoms, and we have to try to name the causes, including explaining what we mean by CanLit. We think the many writers generously lending their voices to this book can light a new way, and we wanted to make this book into a space where that conversation can continue to unfold, as it has already been unfolding, in poetry, journalism, tweets, open letters, and blog posts. Much of that conversation has been immediate and tied to specific controversies, and it is important that it not remain ephemeral within the debates about the state and future of Canadian literature. But the controversies themselves are also a symptom of deeper problems with CanLit and with Canada. *Refuse* works to connect urgent and immediate writing about this moment to long-standing problems in CanLit related to racism, colonialism, sexism, the literary star system, and economic privilege. That is our contribution to this important conversation about writing in Canada.

This isn't the last word on the subject. We hope that it is one contribution of many, and part of a larger conversation that seeks to understand the necessity of structural changes within many cultural industries and institutions.

Refuse as a contribution to debate has several goals. It is a venue for creative and academic writers to think about the recent CanLit controversies in light of the larger issues at stake. The collection also does the work of archiving and preserving important activist contributions that were part of the response to the controversies that have affected CanLit since 2016: notably UBCAccountable, the sexual harassment revelations at Concordia University, the "Appropriation Prize," and debates about Joseph Boyden's identity claims. It is important not to lose that activist work, because many of the most significant interventions took place on social media or were written in ephemeral online venues. This introduction and the introductory material for each section aim to provide background about what has happened to CanLit, and to point out that problems with colonialism, racism, and sexism are not new to the writing, production, and study of Canadian literature. CanLit, to some extent, may even depend on the existence of such problems. That's why we are thinking about CanLit as a formation in ruins. But we are most interested in thinking about how ruins might be figured not only as the ending of something, but also as the beginning of something else.

Living in the Ruins, Staying with the Trouble

In his important 1997 book *The University in Ruins*, Bill Readings says it is too late to save the institution of the university from its newest incarnation as a corporation, at the moment when its status as a symbol of the public good goes into decline. But, he adds, we can "dwell" in the ruins of the university and make something interesting happen, something that works against the university as a corporation but does not yearn for the old days, when universities supposedly mattered to the nation-state. In the ruins, the university "will have to become one place, among others, where the attempt is made to think the social bond without recourse to a unifying idea, whether of culture or of the state."[2] In other words, something new can come from something damaged. We think that CanLit, too, will have to imagine new connections that do not have recourse to a unifying idea of what Canada signifies, or even what it means to write in Canada, now. If CanLit as an institution is in ruins, maybe that's a good thing, even though it is a painful thing for many. These essays and poems point to some of the ways we've reached this place we're calling the ruins, and they do so by thinking through or referencing many of the crises that have broken open CanLit. The contributors think about ways to stay in the ruins of a national literary culture that cannot and should not speak for all, and to learn about other ways of being—and writing—together.

The beginning of living in the ruins inevitably involves recognizing and then mourning what has been lost. As controversies about sexual harassment, neo-colonialism, racism, and industry hierarchies enter mainstream news cycles, it is increasingly impossible to believe that CanLit is an environment where diverse writing, and writers, can flourish. It is time to lose that pervasive, inclusive image of CanLit, because it is clear that CanLit is far from inclusive, or safe, for many of the writers working within it. If we don't own up to what CanLit is and what it does, we risk CanLit being an instance of what Lauren Berlant calls the state of "cruel optimism," which happens when what we desire is an obstacle to our own flourishing.[3] Cruel optimism is about a vague hope that things get better, without the political action needed to actually change what is wrong. It's about hanging on to ideals that will never come to be. If CanLit is a ruin we live within, we have to mourn the ideal of CanLit if we hope to move through it to something better than this.

In the podcast discussion with Jen Sookfong Lee and Dina Del Bucchia cited in this introduction's epigraph, author Katherena Vermette articulated one emotion that is part of the mourning process: sadness. For many of our contributors, there are a lot of sad feelings about this thing we call CanLit. And, as Vermette says, there are a lot of sad feelings about *just fuckin' being alive*—because how we feel about literature and how we feel about the world are, for many of us, inextricable. As we worked to frame this collection of writing, we recognized that thinking about sadness isn't what we'd initially had in mind. And yet, we recognize the feeling of sadness as an important register when we think about what CanLit has meant for many writers, readers, and critics. Sara Ahmed suggests that it is instructive not so much to think about what emotions *are*, but rather what emotions *do*.[4] Ahmed puts it this way when, in reference to her own feminism, she cites Audre Lorde. Lorde's writing taught Ahmed that sometimes it is necessary to stay with difficult emotions or ugly affects that hurt or enrage or sadden you. You have to stay with those emotions long enough to figure out something about yourself and about the world. Many of the contributors to this collection have much to say about being sad about ongoing scandals and injustices found within CanLit. Many are angry, too. That's part of mourning, and both of these emotions have something to teach us.

In a similar fashion, Donna Haraway writes of the possibilities that come of staying with the trouble rather than checking out or turning your back on it.[5] For Haraway, there really isn't an option of checking out of the trouble that is our current global and environmental state, and so she advocates for alternative modes of conceiving of and making kin in order to thrive. She asks us to stay with the trouble rather than pretend it isn't there or think that somehow we can just go back to how things were before the trouble started. In CanLit, there is no "before" the trouble. CanLit as an industry and cultural formation is bound up with the history of Canada as a settler-colonial nation-state. Like the country its writing is supposed to reflect,

CanLit is supposed to be tolerant, liberal, a place where we can imagine our future together. Recent events in CanLit underscore that this is not the case. It has never been the case. *CanLit is in trouble, and it is the trouble.* How do we stay with it, and make new kin?

Staying with the trouble can be an act of care, a way to remember what has happened and a means through which to imagine and build other ways of being together. *Refuse* represents a start to thinking about CanLit in the wake of so many scandals. The contributors write about what those scandals feel like to them, as well as what they can mean. Sadness, anger, rage, ambivalence, and anxiety are here. So, too, are resolve, resilience, resistance, and love. And so we the editors also begin this collection by staying with how it feels to be connected to CanLit for the moment, in order to figure out something of the world of writing and culture in this part of Turtle Island currently called Canada.

Who We Are

We came together to edit *Refuse* because we had been involved in some of the CanLit controversies of 2016 and 2017, as academics, organizers, and public intellectuals. In the aftermath of some of the controversies, and as new ones were beginning, we were part of a 2017 session about UBCAccountable at the annual conference of the Association for Canadian and Québec Literatures. On a very early Sunday morning, the room was full of people who wanted to talk about what was happening to CanLit. As speakers and audience members reluctantly filed out of the room, we felt the need for the conversation to both continue and expand to encompass the necessary contexts of racism, sexism, ableism, and colonialism. The three of us are able-bodied cis white women with stable jobs. We study CanLit and we are editors, but we aren't all creative writers, none of us work in the publishing industry, and we don't share all of the identities and experiences that have been threatened or marginalized by the power structures of CanLit. What could we do to help that conversation happen, without repeating the tendency in CanLit for white, female writers and academics to discipline and domesticate where that conversation goes? How could we provide what scholars can do—context, background, and a long-range perspective about the problems in CanLit—and still highlight what scholarship and creative work can do, together? *Refuse* is the result of that work, deliberately published with an independent press, edited by a collective. We know we run the risk of repeating the work of what is called the "white saviour" paradigm in Canada, where white people are seen as better able to represent the concerns of Indigenous people than Indigenous people can do themselves.[6] White saviours with good, liberal intentions are part of the problem in CanLit, because they can speak over BIPOC (Black Indigenous People of Colour), LGBTQ2S+, and disabled people very easily, and mainstream Canada listens to them more carefully and closely. We came together partly because of our differences in our relation to our individual understandings of "CanLit" and, in generatively and generously discussing those differences, we stayed together to edit this collection because of what became our stronger shared commitment to contribute to changing what "CanLit" has become. We are united in our commitment not to be white saviours. As part of recognizing that there is a long colonial history of such attitudes, we want to share our process as editors for *Refuse*.

One of the more difficult parts of putting this collection together was gathering contributors. These difficulties ranged from recognizing our own limitations to honouring the boundaries of those who refused and the needs of those who said yes. The nature of much of the material *Refuse* addresses is rooted in trauma, and that affected who was able to participate, and how editorial work could proceed. As editors, we understand our work on *Refuse* to be a kind of community-formation and a kind of care-work. Kate Eichhorn and Heather Milne have written of the affective labour of editing, arguing that editorial work is more about attachment to community than monetary compensation.[7] They point out that editing as an act of community curation is not always valued either, and that editors have had to struggle for recognition of this part of their work. But they also write of the politics of curation: any act of collecting is also an act of exclusion. Because we are three white cis women working within universities at different stages of our careers, we inevitably reproduce in this volume the power dynamics that have played out across CanLit, where white women in positions of power select which voices will be heard and which will not. We have elected to do the work of amplifying the writing of contributors, but we do so with the understanding that our very act of editing is a part of the larger systemic issues we are working to address.

As an editorial collective we wrote this introduction together. We developed a method to frame and introduce the essays, poems, and conversations that make up this collection, and we worked to ensure that framing was accountable to contributors. Their contributions make this book what it is, after all. We—Julie, Hannah, and Erin—wrote, edited, and talked *at length* about how to contextualize without overwriting, how to provide inroads for readers new to or unfamiliar with the history (recent and deep) of Canadian literary culture, and how to represent ourselves. We realized in the process of writing that though we share a common vision and common desire to amplify voices as well as try to present a cohesive narrative, we did not in fact see eye-to-eye on everything. Our disagreements and differences of opinion were instructive. They taught us how to discuss more and dismiss less. This kind of critical care is what we have tried to weave into the labour of love that is this collaborative collection.

The Problem of Consensus

When we began to conceive of this book, we imagined it less as an intervention and more as a curation, an archive of the very public and very urgent activist work that has been practised by so many writers, academics, students, and publishers in response to a tangle of events that are recent but have deep roots. We want to use our training as scholars to archive both the work done by writers and cultural critics *and* the work of historicizing. The labour of feminist activism so often goes unarchived, urgent in its moment but forgotten retroactively. How else to explain why Northrop Frye's concept of CanLit as obsessed with the dangers of the wilderness has endured in the public imaginary—along with the garrison-like image of CanLit as a cozy community—while Lee Maracle's act of literally storming the stage at the 1988 Vancouver Writers Festival is rarely discussed?[8]

The official versions of CanLit that are recalled and recirculated are characterized so often by camaraderie and consensus. But an actual look at the history of this cultural institution shows that CanLit isn't about a small pantheon of well-loved celebrity authors, or a series of amusing stories about the empty prairies, or a cozy community of writers. What about (as Lucia Lorenzi wonders) the controversy about the 1994 Writing Thru Race conference, or (as Phoebe Wang asks) the work of writers in the Japanese Canadian Redress movement or (as Keith Maillard suggests) the appropriation controversy and W. P. Kinsella, decades ago? Reflecting on the twentieth anniversary of Writing Thru Race, for example, Larissa Lai shows how much of the radical potential of the event was foreclosed by media coverage in a way that echoes our contemporary moment: "The distinction between barring whites as opposed to radically including First Nations writers and writers of colour for a limited time barely seemed to hit the mainstream forum, and arguments about the history of specific racisms against specific kinds of bodies also barely made it into the public discourse, and certainly was not debated or elaborated in any direct way."[9] How do the fissures that have riven CanLit always seem to be smoothed over and forgotten, as if all the problems are solved?

The problems with CanLit are long-standing, and did not begin with the recent controversies. The events that have occurred in Canadian literary communities in recent years form touchstones for many of the writers here, but the problems with CanLit helped to create the controversies themselves. We need to remember what those problems are, as well as their histories. And we need to re-member, to make a gathering of voices whose work needs to be centred in these conversations moving forward. But first, to understand what kind of ruin we might be living in, we need a better understanding of what "CanLit" means.

What Is CanLit?

The term "CanLit" is used all the time, by writers and others who work in publishing, by academics, by students, and by the media. But does it mean the same thing to all of us? We don't think it does. In fact, we believe that the tensions in CanLit that have arisen in the past three years are in part products of deep divisions found within an industry, a cultural field, and an academic discipline that have, perhaps mistakenly, been given the same name.

In one context, CanLit refers to the academic study of Canadian and Quebec literatures, from pre-Confederation to today. This CanLit has porous boundaries, sometimes including writing in French or other languages besides English, sometimes including writing by Indigenous authors, although the ideology and practice of inclusion is problematic, as some of the contributors to *Refuse* point out. The work of academic CanLit appears in books, edited collections, peer-reviewed journals, conferences, encyclopedias, and online resources. Canadian literature as a subject is taught in secondary and post-secondary institutions in Canada and around the world. It has a canon and is supported by publishing projects like McClelland & Stewart's New Canadian Library imprint as well as anthologies published by trade or academic presses. That canon sometimes, but not always, overlaps with the market success of particular authors and books.

As an industry, CanLit means something different. It describes the apparatus that produces Canadian writing for the market, and it includes the work of writers, editors, small and large presses, journalists, agents, festival workers, bookstores, reading series, juries, reviewers, and more. CanLit is centred on English-language writing, much of it produced for mainstream markets in Canada and internationally. Its dominant genre is that of the literary novel. It is supported by book sales, government grants via the Canada Council for the Arts and other arm's-length organizations, and the work of private and corporate foundations. It has a robust star system and relies heavily on literary prizes for promotion. Creative writing programs in colleges and universities are an important point of entry into CanLit for writers and other industry workers, as well as a source of employment for writers.

To us as editors, CanLit means both the industry and the field of academic study, and their uneven and sometimes unpredictable sites of conflict and contradiction. "Canadian Literature" means literature written and published in Canada. "Literature" includes works of fiction, non-fiction, drama, and poetry that are collectively recognized to have a particular kind of cultural value. We see this as a problem. CanLit discourse in the public sphere sometimes acknowledges the existence of works of journalism, or memoirs, or mass-market mystery writing, or writing for children, or graphic novels, but with the occasional exception that proves the rule, the teaching of and research into these genres is rare. Even the CBC's Canada Reads program focuses overwhelmingly on contemporary fiction, and tends to call that CanLit.[10] CanLit hasn't included much mention of Harlequin romances, even though Harlequin is certainly a great Canadian publishing success story, founded in Winnipeg in 1949 and now, as a division of HarperCollins Canada, selling millions of books internationally each year.

CanLit writ large still clings to a notion of the literary that excludes a lot of the stuff a lot of Canadians like to read because of the work CanLit has been yoked into doing on behalf of Canada, including a rejection of popular culture as a sign of Americanization. As a result, using the term "CanLit" leaves out all manners of communities and histories. For example, "CanLit" does not commonly refer to francophone writing within or beyond Quebec (the academic term "Canadian and Quebec literatures" is meant to point out this problem). The existence of independent francophone and anglophone publishers in Quebec—some with translation programs—still does not often translate into a broad awareness or understanding of francophone writing in English Canada, even when francophone works are translated into English.[11] When it comes to Quebec writing that is widely known, in French or English, Hugh MacLennan's metaphor of "two solitudes" in Canada still exists, and "CanLit" rarely includes it.[12] The existence of an independent publishing industry in Atlantic Canada does not necessarily mean that when CanLit is discussed academically or in the public sphere, the imaginative world of Atlantic Canada exists for other Canadians beyond stereotypical images founded on Anne of Green Gables tourism and fetishizations of folk culture.[13] More to the point, why are so many minoritized authors represented within CanLit only when they tell stories of oppression and marginalization? What about avant-garde experimental work that overlaps with developments in visual art, online performance art, theatre, or music? We learn as much about CanLit from what it leaves out as we do from what is included. This is the CanLit that stands for an overdetermined idea of national literature and the literary industry that supports it.

Writing in Canada—the kinds we might consider literary, as well as other kinds of writing, such as narratives by explorers, diaries by farm women, works about geology or botany, school textbooks, and settler advice manuals—has always been tied to a colonial project of nationhood. And so, when we talk about writing in Canada, and CanLit especially, we are also always talking about the legacy of colonialism here on these lands.

But how did the literary production of/in/about Canada become so centralized, so industrialized, so organized around a notion of national identity? It is no accident, and no coincidence. While we can trace writing in Canada back 150 years or more—and writing on Turtle Island back more than ten thousand years—the contemporary version of CanLit can be linked to the Cold War anxiety about American political annexation, and the resulting Royal Commission on National Development in the Arts, Letters and Sciences (commonly referred to as the Massey Commission) that clearly articulated the need for a distinct national culture as a bulwark against our ravenous neighbours to the south. The 1951 Massey Report led to the formation of the Canada Council for the Arts in 1957, which in turn supported a generation of young writers, many of whom started their own presses, and who then used this efflorescence of publishing to justify, a few decades later, federal support for an independent Canadian publishing industry. At the same time, English-language cultural nationalists fought for Canadian-authored and Canadian-published books to be taught in classrooms; as we mentioned, McClelland & Stewart's New Canadian Library series from 1958 provided affordable course texts for this purpose. New journals like *Canadian Literature* (est. 1959) built up an academic sub-discipline that would turn into university jobs, often occupied by creative writers.

This image certainly is one of coziness and inclusion, with the government and writers and publishers and academics all working together to build a cultural institution that could sustain itself in the face of the greater canonical prestige of British literature (the "classics"), the greater market forces of American publishing (and other forms of popular culture), and a small and dispersed population that is a constant bane to an industry that thrives on scale. But, of course, that narrative is a selective one that imagines out of existence the many writers and thinkers who were actively, deliberately excluded from this new national literature, or included within it as tokens, sometimes presented as evidence of the progressive nature of CanLit itself.

One of the ways that CanLit excludes writers (and genres) is through the very success of its mainstream authors within a complex cultural industry. The production of literature, visual art, television, and dance in Canada are examples of what David Hesmondhalgh calls "the cultural industries."[14] Cultural industries produce intellectual property that can be bought and sold. They provide jobs in an economy not only for cultural producers like writers and artists, but also for publishers, gallery owners, agents, and many others. Unlike most other cultural industries in Canada, CanLit is very big business nationally and internationally, for a very small number of its producers. It has a star system that is used to market the most successful authors beyond Canada's borders,[15] a high-profile system of awards and prizes, and very large multinational publishers, such as Penguin Random House and HarperCollins, that publish authors who are stars or might become stars. Visual art, poetry, dance, and film in Canada contribute to the national imaginary, but a very narrow part of CanLit is also commercially successful. Presenting CanLit as an inclusive community ignores the fact that it is an industry with asymmetrical power relations that have proven hard to shift.

Those power relations may explain why CanLit seems remarkably resistant to all forms of radical social justice when so many of its proponents say they support those principles. The suggestion that CanLit has previously been characterized by "a broadly progressive consensus"[16] is itself deeply ahistorical. Not only has CanLit been marked by a series of similar field-reforming events, from the 1978 Calgary Conference on the Canadian Novel to the 1994 Writing Thru Race conference, but its day-to-day functioning has always been characterized by deep divides and imbalances. Irrevocably imprinted with the sign of the state, funded through initiatives rooted in cultural nationalism, CanLit cannot help but be a profoundly exclusive category, and one whose claims of innateness (CanLit as whatever stories are most Canadian) have been used to police the boundaries of who counts as Canadian and who does not.

At the heart of CanLit as a formation is colonial violence. That violence is what keeps CanLit supposedly open to Indigenous ways of knowing and making knowledge, but in fact closed to anything that would actively dismantle the innate moral authority assumed by its practitioners. In this sense, CanLit is the nation. It articulates the nation to itself and repeats the strategy of inclusion as a way to incorporate opposition into its ideology. Since the mid-nineteenth century, only a select few have been able to fully reap the benefits of national representativeness, and that image of Canada and Canadians has proven remarkably inflexible in its desire to contain, possess, and assimilate the other into itself, whether that other is francophone, Indigenous, disabled, poor, or trans and so on and so on. White women have often been in the vanguard of this kind of moral authority and cultural accommodation in Canada, whether we are talking about Susanna Moodie, Emily Carr, Nellie McClung, L. M. Montgomery, Margaret Laurence, or Margaret Atwood. White women like this get to weigh in on social issues and, in special cases, they get to say who is in or out of the formation.

And how did this happen? Actively. Deliberately. CanLit reflected the nation to itself, and within itself. Because the imagination of what Canada and its literature would be was built on the same foundation of Indigenous genocide, anti-Blackness, anglophone dominance, racist immigration policies, eugenicist attitudes toward disabled people, and deep-rooted misogyny that the rest of Canada was built on. The need for national unity and the long history of CanLit as a bulwark against American imperialism papered over what the foundation of it actually was, and it continues to do so. When Nick Mount, in *Arrival: The Story of Canadian Literature*, says CanLit took Canada "from a country without a literature to a literature without a country,"[17] he is restating a commonly believed proposition that a few 1970s literary celebrities built a literature where there was none before, and then became global successes, just as Canada (at last!) stepped onto the world stage. Like the image of Canada as a place without racism, where tolerance and diversity mark out our national character, this image of CanLit ignores how literary celebrity depended on tokenization and exclusion, of writers and of the environment that made such a narrative of national success so easy to believe.

Rather than thinking of CanLit as only an industry or only an academic area, we are invested in seeing it as a complex cultural formation that includes both these definitions as well as many other, often unnamed, forces and assumptions. Nearly twenty years ago Barbara Godard, drawing on the work of Pierre Bourdieu, wrote about Canadian literature as a "cultural field" in flux, and she pointed to the situation in which we find ourselves now.[18] Godard traced how what we take as given—the social practices and ideas that have histories but become normalized as ahistorical—directly and indirectly influence what a group of people understand as "culture" in a particular geographic space. In Canada, the cultural field prior to the world wars was focused on developing a "national narrative" that, broadly, accounted for settler presences on Indigenous lands. Between the 1950s and the 1990s the cultural field shifted dramatically. It expanded to include home spaces of diasporic writers, and it contracted in the hands of global capital. And so, two decades ago, Godard observed, with the shrinking support for cultural production, a growing awareness of the violent histories of settler colonialism, and an ever-diversifying population, cultural production continued to reflect a particular affective context. In the 1990s Godard saw CanLit reflecting anxiety and worry about its role in the world. Now we see, in glittering award ceremonies and media events, that CanLit has gone global and actively participates in the circulation of cultural and economic capital.

Godard is right to point toward global markets as a central player here. Today we see ever-diminishing support for protectionist forms of cultural nationalism and ever-greater focus on free trade. As an example we might look at the "handover" of McClelland & Stewart, the self-described "Canadian publishers," to multinational publisher Random House in 2011. Now, as of the 2013 merger, that company has become Penguin Random House—itself owned by the larger multinational corporation Bertelsmann. In the midst of these changes, the broader role of CanLit as an industry does less and less to foster an internal sense of cultural identity and more and more to sell that identity to the world. And the identity Canada wants to sell to the world, perhaps best summarized by current prime minister Justin Trudeau, is one of gentle liberalism, polite consensus, and attractively packaged moderate progressiveness. Central to that packaging, in this historical moment, are neo-liberal versions of both feminism and, variously, decolonization or Reconciliation. Unsurprisingly dear to these ideologies are concepts like due process, civility, rule of law, diversity and inclusion, and equality. Antithetical to these ideologies are movements like Idle No More, the 2018 protests against the Trans Mountain pipeline expansion, and the work of Black Lives Matter and #MeToo. These movements position their demands for radical transformation of existing industries and political structures via an understanding of the ongoing workings of colonization, systemic racism, and rape culture.

And so, within the complex cultural field of CanLit, we have a contradiction between a CanLit that profits from the Truth and Reconciliation Commission by turning it into a publishing trend and justifies diversity through sales numbers, literary awards, and celebrity—and an emergent literary culture that builds strength through resistance, refusing to let its diversity be incorporated back into the status quo.

The latest controversies in CanLit blow open these tensions, remind us of their historical significance, and make it difficult to imagine this cultural formation as a cohesive community in which such a contradiction can be easily resolved.

CanLit in Ruins

The current controversies in CanLit can be dated from the formation of the UBCAccountable group. On November 14, 2016, an open letter to the University of British Columbia, signed by eighty-nine writers and CanLit industry figures—many of them well-known and powerful—appeared on a site called UBCAccountable, accompanied by a Twitter hashtag of the same name. The open letter supported novelist and former UBC Creative Writing Program Chair Steven Galloway, who had been fired by UBC after an internal investigation into what it called "serious allegations" about his conduct by a student and other complainants. The text of the letter implied that Galloway, and not the complainants, should be believed and supported. CanLit has been sharply divided about the open letter ever since. Responses to what's been variously referred to as UBCAccountable, the Galloway Affair, or simply the "CanLit Firestorm," have been wide-ranging. As we note above, Simon Lewsen, in *The Walrus*, referred to the event causing "an irreparable generational rift" in a literary community that, "[f]rom the '70s until about two weeks ago, [had] seemed to operate under a broadly progressive consensus." The feminist response to the event, on the other hand, focused on what Kai Cheng Thom, in an essay for *GUTS Magazine*, calls "CanLit Rape Culture."[19] Sexual violence and Indigenous activists on social media first drew attention to the problems of the open letter, followed by a counter-letter petition signed by hundreds of writers, scholars, students, and activists, and other statements and open letters calling on those who signed the UBCAccountable letter to unsign and apologize for what they had done.[20] Many signatories unsigned. Many did not, and took to social media and mainstream publications to argue why Galloway deserves more support than the complainants at UBC. Galloway's appeal of UBC's decision concluded almost one and a half years after the UBCAccountable open letter appeared.[21]

As furor over the UBCAccountable open letter heated up across the country, a second CanLit controversy developed. Novelist Camilla Gibb had already explained in her public Facebook post announcing her decision to remove her signature that she was "guilty of being insecure and susceptible to flattery and the desire for inclusion when a man in a position of power asks."[22] That man in power was Joseph Boyden, who used his celebrity status and position as one of Canada's most successful Indigenous novelists to encourage other writers to sign the UBCAccountable letter. Barely a month after the open letter appeared, *APTN National News* posted an article on

"Author Joseph Boyden's Shape-shifting Indigenous Identity."[23] The article questioned Boyden's claims to Indigenous ancestry and the ways in which he has profited from representing a culture that may or may not be his. Considering the degree to which Boyden's celebrated public status lent support to the UBCAccountable letter, the ties between these two events are evident.

With questions of identity and cultural appropriation in Canadian literature still very much under discussion, the third key event—the "Appropriation Prize" controversy—unfolded in May 2017. Hal Niedzviecki, then editor of the Writers' Union of Canada's *Write* magazine, resigned after publishing an opinion piece called "Winning the Appropriation Prize" in an issue highlighting Indigenous writing in Canada. The authors included in this issue, most notably Alicia Elliott, took justifiable issue with the editorial, which seemed to mock questions of cultural appropriation and Indigenous artistic practice.[24] As Scaachi Koul writes in an article for *BuzzFeed Canada*, "In response, at around midnight on Twitter, a group of white editors, executives, and longtime columnists for some of Canada's largest mainstream publications started collecting money for an 'Appropriation Prize' similar to what Niedzviecki suggested in his piece." Koul adds that the "glibness" with which prominent Canadian media figures—including Ken Whyte, founding editor-in-chief of the *National Post*; Alison Uncles, editor-in-chief of *Maclean's* magazine; and Anne Marie Owens, editor in chief of the *National Post*[25]—responded to Indigenous artists, activists, and intellectuals revealed the neocolonial underpinnings of CanLit itself:

> The conversation was so nakedly cruel, with no shred of possible empathy for people who are really struggling to get their work read, recognized, and appreciated not only by an audience, but by these *exact* editors who act as gatekeepers to said audience. Even more egregious is that this whole argument was rooted in appropriation of Indigenous voices and stories, people who we've taken so much from already.[26]

Mere days later, Rinaldo Walcott, prominent scholar of Black writing and cultural studies in Canada, announced at an academic conference that he was quitting CanLit. As Alicia Elliott cites in her essay for this volume, Walcott was rejecting CanLit's structural and ongoing anti-Blackness, stating: "CanLit fails to transform because it refuses to take seriously that Black literary expression and thus Black life is foundational to it. CanLit still appears surprised every single time by the appearance of Black literary expression and Black life." Walcott's arguments were certainly reinforced in the revelations that past Canadian poet laureate Pierre DesRuisseaux had plagiarized Maya Angelou and Tupac Shakur in his poetry.[27] As scholar Brenna Clarke Gray tweeted on September 12, 2017, this plagiarism was possible because "Black poetry and culture is practically unseen by the powerful in #canlit, who are and who read predominantly white." Anti-blackness intersected with the "two solitudes" problem of poor communication between the cultures of Québec and anglophone Canada, producing an opportunity for rampant appropriation of Black culture. Most commentators refused to acknowledge this.

The revelations about sexual harassment and assault at Canadian creative writing programs continued into 2018, with students of Concordia University's Creative Writing Program filing complaints against professors—revelations that had in fact first been written about in Emma Healey's 2014 article "Stories Like Passwords." Shortly afterwards, former Concordia faculty Mike Spry published the essay "Toxic Masculinity, Concordia, and CanLit" to the URL canlitaccountable.com (a clear reference to the UBCAccountable site), confirming the culture of abuse that permeates university creative writing programs and the Canadian publishing world in general. Within weeks, Scaachi Koul, Marsha Lederman, and other journalists wrote of additional allegations of impropriety in CanLit institutional structures.[28] Most recently, Healey took to Twitter to name her alleged abuser.[29] The intersections of rape culture, anti-Indigenous violence and cultural appropriation, and anti-Blackness seem to permeate CanLit in the twenty-first century. Many of us have known this for as long as we've been working within or at the margins of Canadian literature, whether as writers, publishers, teachers, or some combination of these roles. But this concatenation of events has many asking: is CanLit redeemable, or should we burn it down?

Refusing CanLit

What does it mean to refuse CanLit, to say no to what it stands for, to re/fuse or fire up a different kind of writing by different kinds of writers? What is it like to think about and write in ways that do not support what has come to be called and understood as CanLit? It is, at least in part, to shift the way conversations unfold. Here, in this collection, are contributors working in and outside the academy—scholars and creative writers who have contributed essays, creative non-fiction, poetry, and archival practices. It is moving to see so many contributors thinking through the same issues in different ways, as we all try to stay with the trouble and think about it, together.

Staying with the most recent iterations of "trouble" means, in this collection, staying with what has been unfolding publicly since 2016 and has been referred to by some as a "dumpster fire." The fire imagery is common: in November 2016 journalist Simon Lewsen called the fallout from UBCAccountable a firestorm, and in May 2017 scholar David Gaertner tweeted, in response to Hal Niedzviecki's *Write* editorial, "If this is #CanLit, let it burn." Jen Sookfong Lee and Alicia Elliott both wrote iconic essays in late 2017 referring to it as a "dumpster fire." How might we understand these relatively recent flames within the larger field and history of CanLit itself?

The writers in this collection think through, with, around, and beyond these events in CanLit. They write about the roles they have played in resisting entrenched discrimination in CanLit, and about the intersectionality of the violences of CanLit itself. They imagine other ways to write and publish beyond the events since 2016. Some want CanLit as we know it to come to an end. Some want reform. Some want to point out how this cultural formation never included them to begin with. Some think about how long and deep the fault lines of CanLit are, as long and as deep as the fault lines of Canada itself. Some express love for the writing and writers they care so deeply about. Some look elsewhere and beyond the ruins of CanLit.

Throughout the book, we will continue to do what scholars do most often: offer pieces of context on historical and cultural events, or think about concepts like cultural appropriation. We do this knowing that we are not the last word on what has happened to CanLit, and why, and we know that not everyone who reads this book will agree with our assessment of CanLit.

What is it to refuse? To say no, but also to say yes to something else, to blow up, to fire up.

But also, refuse: garbage, waste, detritus. And, at the same time, re/fuse: to reignite. To think about the fuse. To fuse together. To think about what could be better as we look at CanLit in ruins, just as Bill Readings, in *The University in Ruins*, wrote about what living in the ruins could mean, and the possibilities that such living could hold, without corrosive national ideals at their heart. To live in the ruins, with others, to stay with the trouble and not leave it, that requires an act of love of what writing in this part of Turtle Island could be about. It is a complicated moment to love writing. It is also an incredible moment from which to care, deeply, about how writing and culture work together (or not) to make all sorts of things we call communities. What a good thing to recall, as Zygmunt Bauman reminds us, that though the word *community* is imbued with good feelings, not all communities are healthy, thriving, supported, or strong.[30] Can we think together without reinstating a common national ideal? The writers of *Refuse* ask us to try.

Part One:
REFUSAL

"[Politics consists of] making what was unseen visible; in getting what was only audible as noise to be heard as speech; in demonstrating to be a feeling of shared 'good' or 'evil' what had appeared merely as an expression of pleasure or pain."
— Jacques Rancière, "Ten Theses on Politics"

Any collection that aims to archive a cultural moment must clarify its parameters. Yet, as any writer knows, beginnings are tricky, and, as archivists tell us, marking time is difficult. What gets brought in? What (inevitably) gets left out? And how do we acknowledge the power woven into the very acts of archiving and storytelling? These questions are just a few that kept us up at night wondering how to do justice to the moment as well as the future. The aim, in this first section, is to acknowledge a particular event in the recent history, and to situate that moment in the longer history of literary and cultural production in the history of this settler-colonial nation.

An event is something worth marking—an accomplishment or a passing. The word *event* evokes significance and demands notice. A *rupture event* is an event that interrupts the status quo. A rupture event does not irrevocably rend the fabric of what is, but it does make clear what has been. A rupture event is political in the sense that, as Jacques Rancière suggests, it makes what was unseen visible. Idle No More. Black Lives Matter. #BeenRaped-NeverReported. #MeToo. These are all rupture events insofar as they insist on mainstreaming "what was only audible as noise to be heard as speech." There is risk in rupture. As Leanne Betasamosake Simpson observed in a 2018 conversation with Dionne Brand, mainstreaming for a "wider audience" "is code for white audience, which is code for less angry, less political, more palatable."[1] There is risk and there is possibility in refusing the mainstream version of events and exploring what rupture events could signify instead.

This opening section of *Refuse: CanLit in Ruins* marks a rupture in CanLit—both the industry and the institution—as a starting point for thinking about refusal as a form of rupture. The catalyst was the publication, on November 14, 2016, of the UBCAccountable open letter to the University of British Columbia.[2] To the surprise of some UBCAccountable supporters, the letter was not well-received, and powerful writers were not able to convince CanLit and the Canadian public that they were right. Controversy erupted as writers, professors, students, journalists, and members of the public rose up in opposition to the letter's support of Galloway and lack of mention of the students and others who had registered complaints against him, making plain that issues connected to sexual harassment in creative writing programs—and in CanLit itself—had to be discussed openly. Instead of consensus, many refused the arguments of the UBCAccountable letter. Some went on to resist the status quo in CanLit itself and challenge other problems within it to do with colonialism, sexism, ableism, class, and racism. In the words of these commentators, CanLit becomes, in Rancière's terms, political because what had been audible only as "noise" became speech and what had been unseen became visible. And what was visible—at first—was refusal. The events of 2016 and 2017 mark one of the key cultural moments of recent history that serve as an important event in the longer history of literary production, cultural celebrity, and the relationship between creative writing in and outside academic spaces.

The contributors to this opening section take up refusal as a galvanizing mode of action. Here, naming, archiving, and historicizing become tools for refusal. Here, refusal is enacted through naming different sorts of power. Here, refusal is explored as a means of moving forward without reproducing the same inequities of the past. Refusal of what? Of discourses of certain kinds of power. The pieces in "Refusal" archive events and conversations that unfolded on digital platforms from November 2016 onward, using narrative as a means to contextualize what happened, and what the controversy signifies. For example, in her contribution, writer and scholar Tanis MacDonald asks what CanLit and class have to do with each other. She points out that the silent work of class is at play throughout the history of cultural production in this country, whenever debates about what will "count" as national literature come to the forefront. We might take note, for example, of how working-class literary forms like pulp magazines have been "stigmatized as both a form of lower-class literature and a form of American mass culture," as Michelle Denise Smith argues.[3] Or we could look to how popular middle-class literary forms like sentimental poetry, from Edna Jacques to Rupi Kaur, have been sneered at by a literary elite largely located in universities. Class is always at play when we decide what "counts" as literature and what doesn't. But class is also at play when power and cultural capital attach themselves to particular successful individuals—celebrities, we call them—in ways that grant those individuals the ability to decide who is out and who is in.

In the public withdrawal of her signature from the UBCAccountable letter, author Camilla Gibb signalled the role that both celebrity and gender played in her initial decision to sign. What she says is worth repeating: "I am also guilty of being insecure and susceptible to flattery and the desire for inclusion when a man in a position of power asks. Despite being almost 50. Despite being established. Because I am still a woman."[4] Gibb's statement signals a rupture—she puts into language what is explained away as ephemeral, emotional, and subjective. In their creative essay, Jane Eaton Hamilton represents a different take on this issue, examining the everyday nature of arguments about believing those who report, and affirming why it is essential that feminists believe what survivors have to say. The #MeToo movement has used quantitative data to make its arguments. There is no denying that data is compelling and convincing. In their essay, Hamilton adds to the importance of data in making arguments about social and structural change by emphasizing the necessity of listening to survivors and believing that they are the experts on their own experiences.

A significant part of the resistance to the rupture events of 2016 and 2017 did not take place in mainstream media outlets such as *The Walrus* or major newspapers, but rather in online blogs and on the social media platforms Facebook and Twitter. Twitter in particular had already been a site for discussions about another open letter in defence of Steven Galloway, by author Madeleine Thien.[5] The platform subsequently became an important place for information-sharing and debate about the controversy because the initial UBCAccountable intervention included the discussion thread #ubcaccountable. At first, the hashtag was used by open-letter signatories to promote their points of view and link to the website accompanying the letter. Very quickly, sexual violence activists, Indigenous activists, and others who opposed or questioned the letter and its function used the thread as well, and a lively debate ensued. Men's Rights Activists and anti-feminist trolls joined the thread later, and most traffic via the #ubcaccountable thread ceased.

There is another important reason why so much of the debate about CanLit controversies took place online. The hierarchical nature of the industry and institution of CanLit means that very few writers and commentators beyond some stars have access to mainstream media outlets. High-profile signatories were able to give interviews and write op-eds for major publications, but most other commentators did not have the same access, and so blogs and social media platforms became the only way for other writers and activists to join the debate. The ephemeral nature of social media in particular means this kind of labour is easily lost. Kim Goldberg's contribution to the resistance, as she kept track of who signed and unsigned the UBCAccountable open letter and posted the results on Twitter, is an excellent example of this necessary work, so vital and too often, unsung and unseen.

The first contribution in this section is an essay posted to the now-defunct website Storify by anthropologist and activist Zoe Todd on November 16, 2016. In it, Todd frames her critique in terms of the intersecting and overlapping forces of rape culture, colonialism, and white supremacy. She particularly calls upon author Joseph Boyden, the initial public voice for the open letter, to reconcile his position with his work on Missing and Murdered Indigenous Women. The question of Boyden's Indigeneity was raised frequently during the conversations that followed, including calls to accountability by many Indigenous women, Todd among them. These calls to accountability can be linked to revelations that emerged not long afterwards about Boyden's claims of Indigenous identity. Amongst other things, Todd's essay is a reminder of how many conversations about CanLit unfold through social media—especially Twitter and Facebook—where perspectives and voices that may not have access to mainstream media platforms can critique and intervene. The Métis feminist orientation of Todd's work reminds us to take Twitter seriously as a platform for cultural criticism, even as we recognize the toxic and exploitative dimensions of the site.

Novelist and poet Keith Maillard has taught in UBC's Creative Writing Program since 1989.[6] His contribution connects the events at the university to the 2017 cultural appropriation controversy and the cultural appropriation debate of the 1980s and 1990s. In so doing, Maillard points to another relatively recent era of cultural appropriation in CanLit that was rooted in the manifestation of power imbalances.

Power is both difficult to see and, often, more difficult to articulate clearly. Lucia Lorenzi's essay challenges us not only to reckon with the history of CanLit as an institution structured by multiple forms of oppression and exclusion, but also to think about how contemporary institutions are complicit with the perpetuation of rape culture. In a historical moment that will certainly be remembered for the explosive virality of activist Tarana Burke's #MeToo on social media and escalating revelations of assault alleged against prominent figures like Harvey Weinstein, many industries are experiencing their own rumblings. In a 2018 article for *The Walrus*, author Zoe Whittall noted that CanLit is struggling to deal with its sexual-harassment problem because "[in] Canada, our famous and powerful literary elite are focusing on due process."[7] Fixation on a narrow idea of due process is one of the features of rape culture that Whittall highlights, alongside skepticism toward data on the widespread nature of sexual harassment and assault, overinflation of the frequency of false accusations (what Whittall calls a "present-day mythology"), and a tendency for people to claim they "believe women" until that belief challenges prevailing power structures or personal relationships. Lorenzi's essay makes it clear that rape culture cannot be isolated from the other manifold violences of CanLit. Instead we must learn to account for it, and be accountable for it, alongside the other forces—including colonialism, white supremacy, ableism, and homophobia—with which sexual violence intersects.

The contributions in this first section consider, contextualize, and address a few recent rupture events from multiple angles. The conclusions they draw are singular, but they share a common undercurrent: in a settler-colonial nation with a history of enslavement and the ongoing disavowal of justice for all, there can be only refusal as a means to move forward.

Rape Culture, CanLit, and You

ZOE TODD

Some collated tweets regarding the letter signed by the CanLit who's who calling for an investigation of how UBC handled investigation into allegations re Steven Galloway.

I start this storify by stating: all university investigations of allegations of sexual misconduct, sexual harassment, bullying, and other matters that involve students are traumatizing. These processes are impersonal and invasive. They leave a lot of trauma in their wake. I understand why Joseph Boyden has, as reported in the *Vancouver Sun* on November 15, 2016, spearheaded efforts to call for an investigation into the most recent high-profile case of a Canadian university terminating someone in relation to serious allegations:

> "The publisher for author Joseph Boyden confirmed he spearheaded a group effort to write and circulate the open letter, although not all those on the list could be reached to confirm their support. Boyden, who is the author of the award-winning novel 'Through Black Spruce,' sent an email to writers asking for their signatures, saying the open letter 'does not draw conclusions about guilt or innocence, but focuses on a process that ill-served complainants and Mr. Galloway.'"[1]

However, there are ways to condemn that process that also make room to stand in solidarity with the students who came forward and who were traumatized by the process as well. Despite being authored by the top writers in the country, this letter does not achieve this. Instead, it uses language like "unsubstantiated" and points to the fact that no criminal charges were laid in the case. Well, I hope Canadian Literati remember the incredible burden of proof that is put upon survivors of sexual harassment, sexual assault, and harassment or bullying in the workplace. There is a reason that up to two out of three rapes goes unreported.[2]

It is also important to note that the lack of criminal charges in a case like this is not necessarily an exoneration. As you well know, the burden of proof in cases like this is very high. All Canadians learned this this spring with the Ghomeshi trial.

> Tweet from @ZoeSTodd: "Do @MargaretAtwood @MiriamToews @josephboyden know of Val D'or where no charges were laid. Letter for police, too?[3]

I am a professor. My job, first and foremost, is to teach. And to extend a significant duty of care to my students. I, too, stand firmly opposed to processes that traumatize or revictimize students. I stand firmly with efforts to build departments and faculties where exploitation of students is not allowed. I stand firm in efforts to end rape culture on our campuses, and I stand firm with survivors whose stories are not heard, who are forced to continue working in spaces where sexual abusers and those who perpetrate assault are never brought to justice. The statistics offered to professors in Ontario from surveys of student mental health indicate incredible levels of anxiety and depression amongst undergrad and graduate students. There are ongoing conversations happening at many universities about the role that heteropatriarchy (and, yes, sexual harassment) play in this current state of things. Further, current high-profile cases of (repeat) sexual misconduct at universities like Berkeley and Yale teach us that these issues go all the way to the top of our fields. This issue at UBC was being weighed in the context of an endemic, widespread, and *continuously reaffirmed* order of sexual harassment and misogyny across all university spaces. This, too, must be investigated.

So, in response to the substantive points of the letter, I think it is important here to refer back to this statement from UBC issued in response to the letter—Mr. Galloway's termination is being reviewed by UBC through his (necessary and important) right to grievance:

Tweet from @EmilyLazatin980: "Statement from @UBC on writers asking for independent investigation into Steven Galloway affair." [Posted 7:16pm, 15 Nov 2016]

Text of statement: UBC acknowledges recent concerns raised about its handling of the case concerning Mr. Steven Galloway, including those expressed by a number of Canadian authors in the Globe and Mail on November 15. When there is significant public interest in a private employment matter, it creates difficulties for all the parties involved, including Mr. Galloway, the complainants, who were students at UBC, and the university.

We would like to take this opportunity to confirm our commitment to fairness and to shed some more light on the decision-making processes followed in such matters. UBC reached its decision only after a thorough, deliberative process conducted in accordance with the requirements of the B.C. Labour Relations Code, the B.C. Freedom of Information and Protection of Privacy Act, and UBC's collective agreement with the UBC Faculty Association, the union representing faculty members.

In response to a call from the authors for an independent review of how UBC handled this employment matter, it is important to note that a review of the university's decision is already underway. Like any former faculty member, Mr. Galloway has the right to challenge the university's decision and the Faculty Association has filed a grievance and arranged for senior legal counsel. His grievance will be heard by an independent and experienced arbitrator that UBC and the Faculty Association have mutually agreed upon.

UBC remains bound by privacy law from detailing the allegations against Mr. Galloway unless he waives his right to privacy, which he has not done. Confidentiality is a critical underpinning of UBC's review processes not only for the respondent, but also for complainants, who are often vulnerable and concerned for their academic and professional careers. However, we can reassure those who have raised concerns that the allegations will be tested again through an independent arbitration, agreed to by the UBC Faculty Association and the university.[4]

What I think is most important here is for the prominent, celebrated Canadian authors who have signed this letter so far to understand the cultural power this letter has and its (I imagine unintended) silencing power over those in the Canadian Literature community who have experienced, or who are experiencing, sexual violence, violence, and abuse within this small, tight-knit Canadian arts, media, and literature community. Focusing so intently on Mr. Galloway's experience without tending to the experiences of the students and complainants in this case has the powerful effect of, as one person tweeted, "intimidating survivors."

Tweet from @marshalederman: "Complainant on CanLit open letter re Steven Galloway: 'It reads like Canada's most powerful authors saying be quiet'" [Posted 7:32pm, 15 Nov 2016][5]
Link to article: "UBC responds to criticism over firing of Steven Galloway"[6]

So I turn here to addressing the person who spearheaded this letter, Mr. Boyden. As an Indigenous woman professor, as someone who has experienced extensive harassment (misogyny, racism) in the academy in the past for speaking out about racism and misogyny in our classrooms and conference hallways, and as someone whose first duty is to stand in solidarity with students who face incredible barriers to support and due process when they *do* face harassment of all kinds in the academy, I have to ask Mr. Boyden how he can reconcile his role in spearheading this letter in its current form (specifically the way it is written, such that it excludes any acknowledgement of the trauma the complainants have faced) with his very public writing and support of issues regarding Missing and Murdered Indigenous Women, Girls and Two-Spirit Persons, including your role in editing the book *Kwe*. Joseph, the message your letter sends is that survivors are an afterthought. Your letter makes Indigenous women in Canadian literature and scholarly spaces feel unsafe. The signatories to the letter are now a list of people who Indigenous women in Canadian literature and arts cannot trust to dismantle heteropatriarchy in the spaces where we hit the glass ceiling with such unfailing frequency. As several people noted on Twitter, where were the letters of support and outrage when issues of misogyny and exploitation in Canadian Lit came to light in 2014, 2015, or even other cases throughout 2016? If you are going to stand in solidarity with Steven Galloway and his treatment by UBC stemming from the allegations raised by people within his department, then you must exert incredible care in ensuring that you *also* stand in solidarity with people who face ongoing abuse within all facets of Canadian Lit. Because, again, two out of three rapes go unreported. And the Ghomeshi trial teaches us that coming forward with reports of abuse at the hands of prominent Canadian glitterati is a traumatizing matter, one very likely to be dismissed by Canadian courts.

So, I believe her. I believe them. I stand with those ending rape culture. I acknowledge the violence of university processes for handling allegations of sexual misconduct and workplace harassment. I can assert that while also acknowledging the disenfranchisement of students in these systems and processes. And I hope the signatories to this letter realize what damage they have done to emerging writers who work hard to build up safe, nurturing, and accountable spaces for our work across this country. This letter and its failure to tend to the experiences of complainants underscores our need to End Rape Culture. Everywhere.

At the end of the day, we must recognize that while university processes for investigating serious allegations are inherently flawed, we must acknowledge this is because they are embedded in a white supremacist, heteropatriarchal, and, yes, settler-colonial academic system in Canada that operates to reproduce itself against the lives of those it exploits. A meaningful letter from our CanLit heroes could have started off with an acknowledgement of the pressures and struggles that emerging writers face across the country, of the competition and anxiety that is endemic to chronically underfunded writing and arts programs, of the shifting landscapes of CanLit under, first, the Harper regime and now our growing fears about the impact Trump will have on marginalized peoples across North America. The letter could have acknowledged the previous examples where survivors have spoken out about abusive and exploitative dynamics within CanLit and the tight-knit fields of Canadian arts/culture. It could have started by saying, "We acknowledge that rape culture is real and for these reasons we feel that universities like UBC must completely overhaul how they deal with serious allegations of sexual misconduct." It should have started, in other words, with a nod to the fact that sexual harassment and violence and misogyny are very real experiences for many Canadian writers. And then it could have tended to the experience of the writer involved in this most recent investigation at UBC. But it did not. It did not. And now, this letter sits with us. Heavy, silencing. And protecting a very well-shielded CanLit status quo.

BURN

KEITH MAILLARD[1]

As Alicia Elliott wrote in September 2017 and for this volume, CanLit is a raging dumpster fire. That fire could not have burned with such fury if the flammable material inside hadn't been piled up so high.

The injunction #Believewomen means not only believe them about specific cases but believe them when they say things like, "*I told you. This shit's been going on for years.* In Hollywood, in academia, in CanLit—"

Emma Healey: "Once you say it out loud, doors start to open." Her essay, "Stories Like Passwords," was published in 2014.[2]

🔥

Because of privacy legislation the University of British Columbia cannot release the Boyd Report, so we have no way of knowing if the report referred to and quoted in Madeleine Thien's original letter to UBC, published in the *Globe and Mail*,[3] Kerry Gold's article in *The Walrus*,[4] or the original UBCAccountable open letter could be genuine or be an edited, cherry-picked, or even fabricated version.

🔥

According to Madeleine Thien in her letter to UBC: "[W]hen it comes to criminal and violent acts, I personally believe UBC and Creative Writing had a human and civic obligation to inform the police ... [W]e must invoke and use the legal system, even when it is flawed..." This argument—and we continue to hear it frequently—betrays a profound ignorance of rape culture. Most sexual assaults are never reported; those that are reported rarely make it to court; those that do make it to court rarely result in justice for the complainant. Many women have told us that going through the legal system is more traumatic that the original assault.

◆

No one who has felt so free to comment—not Madeleine Thien, not Margaret Atwood, not Joseph Boyden—not any of the signatories of the #UBCAccountable letter—not any of the others who have held forth with such self-righteousness on Twitter and Facebook—not a single one of them knows anything whatsoever about what actually happened. One would think, in cases in which one knows absolutely nothing, the best thing to do would be to keep one's mouth shut. If, however, one were merely to follow the feminist injunction #believewomen, one would be right well over 90 per cent of the time.

Many of those #UBCaccountable signatories might consider themselves to be progressive, more left than right. Many might even consider themselves to be feminists. Many might say: "*Of course I believe women*—" Well, except when the accused happens to be a friend of a friend. Well, except when the accused is a member of a very exclusive club and the signatory is proud to be part of it.

◆

It would be difficult to overestimate the devastation caused by the #UBCaccountable letter. It sent a clear and persuasive message to young and emerging writers, telling them that if they dared to come forward with a complaint about any member of the exclusive #Canlit club, the entire weight of that club would come down on their heads and crush them out like bugs.

◆

"Some things I can't talk about because I'm bound by privacy legislation," I told an undergraduate class at UBC, "but other things I can. Don't be afraid to talk to me, and don't be afraid to talk to each other."

Half the class didn't have a clue what I meant, but the other half did. There was an intense buzz as they tried to explain it to each other. One of those who knew summarized it for one of those who didn't: "Margaret Atwood hates us."

🔥

At the height of the controversy, an extraordinarily vile Men's Rights Activist website created several videos telling lies about UBC Creative Writing. Some of the complainants who had been mentioned in Thien's letter were targeted and named on that site. One of the female faculty at my institution, UBC, was subjected to a sprightly little tune that had as its chorus, "You're a cunt." MRA are alt-right, with thousands of anonymous followers who can flood targeted people with hate messages, including rape threats and death threats. It is disconcerting to see the author of *The Handmaid's Tale* claimed as an ally and praised on an MRA website.

🔥

Writing in *ABCBookworld* (abcbookworld.com) about the early days of UBC Creative Writing, Andreas Schroeder tells us "there was always plenty of chaos in the department. One contributing factor—quite widespread throughout the university in those days—was the practice of professors sleeping with students. Somehow, nobody seemed to think that was a problem..."

I, too, remember the late sixties and early seventies, when it was commonly thought that sex was good for you, when a standard line men used to get women into bed was to call them "uptight and repressed." Looking back on it, I would say now that sex was probably good for the men. If you want to know what the women thought, ask them.

🔥

When I was hired at UBC on tenure track in 1989, George McWhirter, the head of our program then, made it utterly clear that the good old days were long over. It was an unwritten protocol in Creative Writing that professors did not become sexually involved with students.

🔥

In November of 2016, Kyla Jamieson, one of our MFAs, tweeted:

> some say there's a struggle for control in ubccrwr and it's true
> it's Old School vs. Everyone Else and it's not a new struggle but thx
> for finally tuning in

🔥

The old right-left breakdown no longer works, and a new alignment has taken place. It's a gender split, but not entirely. It's a generational split, but not entirely. It's pretty much Old School vs. Everyone Else.

🔥

I'm a settler white guy, so my opinion as to whether or not Joseph Boyden is Indigenous doesn't matter a damn, but I was very interested in what Indigenous people had to say, so I retweeted many of them to amplify their voices.

In a mixture of fascination and horror I watched in real time as some of the most powerful people in Canadian media made jokes about starting an "Appropriation Prize."

🔥

When he was writing them, W. P. Kinsella called them "Indian stories." He wrote seven volumes of them and referred to them as a "goldmine." White people liked these stories, found them fun and amusing. *The Fencepost Chronicles* won the Leacock Medal for Humour in 1987.

Kinsella was a fervent defender of "free speech," saying repeatedly that a fiction writer was free to write anything he damn well pleased. In an interview with *ABCBookWorld* (1985–86) on abcbookworld.com, he said, "No, I've never been on the reserve at Lac Ste. Anne... I've never been to Hobbema either. I don't want to go. Because everything I write is fiction. I don't want to be confused by fact."

🔥

One of the reasons Kinsella's "Indian" characters were so popular with white people was that they are stock figures from the old-time minstrel shows — Amos 'n' Andy for Canadians.

Kinsella built his career by making up "Indians." He's one of many white writers who have done that. Since they first got off the boat, white people have been making up "Indians."

Kinsella's made-up "Indians" have been absorbed into the culture and contribute to what white people think they know about Indigenous people. Writers make up the reality in which we live.

❀

Kinsella's campaign for "free speech" is still very much alive: the term has become a buzzword signalling the presence of the alt-right.

Free speech does not mean that anyone can say anything they want and not be criticized for it. Free speech does not mean that a university—or anyone else, for that matter—is required to provide a platform.

Some stories we are uniquely positioned to tell. Other stories are not ours to tell because it is unlikely we will ever have the time and energy to do the work necessary to make them ours.

❀

"Positionality" is a term I recently learned from one of my students. Back in the sixties we called it "where I'm coming from."

For me, writing and reading have always been two faces of the same thing—an ongoing conversation. To understand who I was and where I was, I needed to be part of that conversation. It was a matter of survival.

If you never see anyone like yourself represented in stories—and I didn't—it's difficult to feel like part of the human race. Eventually it occurred to me that if I wanted to see stories about people like me, I would probably have to write them myself.

I was active in the US anti-war movement in the late sixties, and most of the women I knew became involved in what was then called "women's liberation." They were talking about the things I had always been thinking about, but a woman friend told me in the kindest way to stop trying to be part of their movement. "We women have to do it ourselves," she said. "Go organize in your own community."

I understood perfectly why women had to do it for themselves, but as to organizing in my own community, that was a different matter. *What* community? I had never in my adult life considered myself to be a straight man—or, as I would say now that the term has become available, I have never self-identified as cis gender. So I organized in my own community by writing *Two Strand River* with its gender-switched protagonists. That was my bid to alter reality.

Because writing creates reality, it is a sacred act. The stories submitted by creative writing students are sacred texts.

🔥

The thought of priests sexually abusing members of their congregation is so horrifying because priests hear confessions. It is generally accepted that doctors, psychiatrists, psychologists, and therapists should not have sex with their clients, and in all of those professions there are clearly stated rules creating proper boundaries. In creative writing workshops, the students are particularly vulnerable: they are putting their souls on paper. We need clearly stated rules to protect them.

🔥

With the amalgamation of the big Canadian publishers and their increasing emphasis on volume of sales, old-school #Canlit has converted itself into a branch of the entertainment industry. I have nothing against being entertained, but when I want to read something that matters, I will look elsewhere. The complex network of power relationships exemplified by the signatories of the #UBCAccountable letter is becoming increasingly irrelevant.

🔥

Nearly fifty years ago, the American poet Gary Snyder wrote that "[the] 'free world' has become economically dependent on a fantastic system of stimulation of greed which cannot be fulfilled, sexual desire which cannot be satiated and hatred that has no outlet except against oneself, the persons one is supposed to love, or the revolutionary aspirations of pitiful, poverty-stricken marginal societies... They [modern societies] create populations of 'preta'— hungry ghosts, with giant appetites and throats no bigger than needles. The soil, the forests and all animal life are being consumed by these cancerous collectivities; the air and water of the planet is being fouled by them."

Those hungry ghosts with their giant appetites have revealed themselves by now. They built their wealth by regarding people as property. They maintain a worldview that regards women as prey, Indigenous people as obstacles to be removed, murdered, or assimilated, and mother earth as a female body to be exploited for profit.

🔥

Burn.

The You Know

JANE EATON HAMILTON

He called it *The You Know. The Incident. The Situation.*

I had the idea he was pumping me for what I had learned about *The You Know* or what I was willing to divulge, which in the first case was nil, which negated the second case. I was in the thick of it because I'd invited Complainant X to open for me at an event, but what nobody had realized was that I hadn't known Complainant X was Complainant X. The truth was, I'd invited her for literary reasons, but if I'd known she was Complainant X, I'd have invited her sooner.

I minded my own p's and q's.

What my interlocutor didn't understand was that I objected on feminist grounds, not personal ones. I hadn't met the guy. I hadn't read the guy's writing. I didn't care about the guy one way or another.

The guy was a guy like any guy was a guy to me.

You know? Big whoop. Take the guy in question and throw him into a guy-pile and shake. Spit one random guy out and, whoever it was, if he behaved like a venomous snake, well, my results would not vary. If he didn't behave like a venomous snake, well then, we might be friends.

I mean, men had been lying about sexual crimes for so many decades (centuries) that I had to either believe there were no crimes of sexual harassment and assault, or disbelieve men. I looked at what a womxn could lose versus what a man could lose. She lied to get into trouble and he told the truth to stay out of it vs. she told the truth to get into trouble and he lied to get out of it?

Men, themselves, did not appear as a gender to be credible.

My interlocutor said that Complainant Y was "fa—" but then realized he'd stumbled because I was fat and so his eyes went wide, and instead he said Complainant Y had a "real presence. I mean," he said, trying to backtrack, "you knew when she entered a room that she was a real seductress. My wife took one look at her and said, *Here comes trouble.*"

I was not free to roll my outside eyes, but I rolled my inside eyes. "You prejudged her?"

I had prejudged that the food in the restaurant would be next to inedible, but I'd ordered some of it anyhow. A waitress in a bilious-pink uniform slid thick plates in front of us.

"I didn't prejudge her," he said. "I just knew. My wife knew. And we were right. We told the guy not to get involved with her."

"Do you like this food? This food is crap," I said. It seemed the right kind of food for Squamish. I ate fries. He ate salad.

The You Know was just a small slithering part of *You Know What the World Is Like For Womxn.*

"I think *The You Know* hates womxn," I said.

"I think you hate men," he said. "If it's true you don't know him and you haven't read him, then I don't see why you'd go after him."

"Believing womxn is not the same thing as going after him."

"But you say you don't know the victims! I'm saying I know them. They have histories. I'm saying I know she's lying."

"You were there?"

"You are frustrating to talk to." He stared at me. "She's, like, so curvy." He made the figure with his hands as if he was a man from 1955.

"You can't do that. You can't just pick things like that, as if sexy people lie and it's a proven research fact. That people who are sexy can't get sexually assaulted."

"I'm a feminist."

"Feminists don't say, *But he's such a great guy; he's been my best friend since ever. If you just knew him like I do* ... Because you *don't* know him like the victims do. You can't, if he didn't offend against you."

"No, geez, of course not. Don't be stupid. He didn't touch my wife." He had frizz instead of hair on top of his head. "Don't look at me like that. I'm a guy."

The You Know made the air in the restaurant needly. It suddenly felt like vaccinations.

"You see?" I waited, but he just gobbed iceberg lettuce into his mouth. "But just because he didn't doesn't mean he didn't offend against someone else, right? Surely you see that? Feminists know there's a vast history of illegal and unethical sexual behaviour and that systems exist to keep it happening."

He stabbed the radishes like they had personally attacked him. "Maybe in most cases you say that, but ..." He smiled a big smile at me. "Okay, I'm not a feminist feminist."

"But he was known to be kind of a dick, right? Didn't he do other questionable things, things students witnessed?"

"Maybe. Sort of. Yeah. There are some things."

"Well, I mean, if he did not-actionable things that were still, like, creepy, doesn't that sort of imply you should believe what the complainants are saying?"

"Well," he said, "but those other things, those women were not complainants." His shoulders slumped and he leaned toward me. He said he'd tell me something. He straightened. The Alleged Offender had lied. He'd caught him lying not about the Alleged Offences, but about something else, something small and inconsequential. But, on the other hand, he said wearily, he'd caught Complainant Y in a fib. So who really knew? Who could know? Who could ever know?

"Sexual assault stats know," I said. "In study after study—and not studies run by feminists—only 2 to 8 per cent of victims fabricate. What kind of total schmuck would your friend have to be to have grabbed all those statistical liars just for himself?"

"They deserved each other, those two, is all I can say," he said, dragging a napkin across his lips, "the Alleged Offender and Complainant Y. So I'm calling it a draw." He shrugged, sighed. "Also, listen. Complainant Y, she . . . she did this thing."

"What thing?"

"This thing with his, well, with something else in his life." He explained a complicated identity theft. "She wanted to ruin him. There was no doubt."

"Assuming that's true, surely you could want to ruin somebody and still have had a crime committed against you? How are those two mutually exclusive?"

"Because she's vile."

"But you can be vile and still have been harassed or raped, surely?"

"Completely vicious," he said, shaking his head.

"Well, maybe the Alleged Offender pretended to be Complainant Y and hacked himself, and set her up? Did you ever consider that?"

My idea was not to change his mind, but to disturb his certainty.

The community was spliced down the middle, some on one side of *The You Know* and the rest on the other side of *The You Know*, where the Alleged Offender stood pontificating with his pals. Powerful people stood with the Alleged Offender. If you lined them up, there wouldn't be enough supporters to cross a city, because most people in CanLit acted like they were neutral, like Switzerland, but there were enough of them to stretch around a block. There were benefits, whole careers at stake—festival invitations, grants, agents, publishers. One writer freaked people out by saying there would be "consequences" but didn't say what they'd be.

We got the message, all of us uppity folks.

There were consequences to standing with the Alleged Offender as well, I guessed. Trouble sleeping. Anxiety. A worry about their side of history. Small hard pieces of coal in the pits of stomachs. Worry that people wouldn't want to read them any longer, that profs would see how the wind was blowing and remove them from curricula. The terrible feeling that is self-righteousness or the need to face-save.

I said, "I won't read any of those writers again. I won't buy their books. I've mostly taken them off my shelves. I put their books in recycling rather than give them to small libraries or thrift stores."

"That's punitive," he said. "That's *mean*."

"Well, you know, they can do the same with my books." I ate some fries. They tasted like cardboard. I laughed. "I'll bet none of them ever bought my books, because it never was a two-way street, was it, where I read them and they read me. Where I supported them and they supported me. Uh-uh, nope, it wasn't." I looked up at the fans. It was too cold in the restaurant. "Maybe I'm a petty bastard, but there again, I want to give my money to writers who lift up rather than push down. I mean, isn't reading those writers now like watching movies by Woody Allen? There are a lot of great books out there by marginalized people. I could read nothing else for the rest of my life and have a very fulfilling reading life."

I said I was worried about the long term, about the careers of the Complainants, about other students who would be scared to disclose harassment and sexual assaults now. "It's like his friends want us to go back to the days when the perp was the victim and the victim was the perp."

By now, *The You Know* looked like it had been shredded in a dryer. It waved above us in the air, like zombie ectoplasm dripping its toxins.

"We really can't resolve this," he said, pushing his plate away. "I'm sorry you don't like me."

"It's not whether I like or don't like you. It's not personal. It's that I think your position does harm to womxn and makes their futures harder. Even your own kids' futures, if they ever need future help."

He scowled at how mean this was, but maybe he'd consider it, later, that the womxn affected were as real as his children. He said, "We can't fix this. You know what you know and I know what I know."

That was indisputably true, except that I really knew nothing.

"What students would report if they knew the leaders in their field were going to try to discredit them? There is already far too much discrediting of victims going on. I don't want womxn to shut up just because of

The You Know. I've fought all my life to give womxn back their voices. I want womxn to roar. I want womxn to be bigger and stronger and more fierce still."

He rolled his eyes.

"I hope Complainant Y comes out of this taking up even more space."

"No, you don't!" and he laughed. He sobered up and slapped his napkin down. "Here's the thing: you can't go around maligning the Alleged Offender."

"But I don't malign him. I malign sexual assault. I malign power dynamics that infringe on students' rights. As I said, I don't even know him."

"They're going to sue you," he said.

This was the sort of threat *The You Know* generated. I'd heard it frequently.

"You can sue anybody for anything until a judge turfs it out. But for what kind of victory?"

He made a sound like he knew what kind of victory, and it was a victory I wouldn't like.

"They'd just sound like dicks in court and then that, too, would go in CanLit's permanent record. Plus they'd hurt me, an ill senior, and my kids, and my grandkids, too, and all of us would tell the story about *that* for generations."

"I can't talk to you."

"No, I know. You really can't." I pushed away my plate. *The You Know* was not nourishing.

"See?"

"I do see."

The server slipped our cheques onto the table.

We paid *The You Know*'s bills. My interlocutor was unhappy and I was unhappy and *The You Know* was just *The You Know*, always bitterly, rapaciously itself. We tipped even though *The You Know*'s food sucked; that wasn't the server's fault. Part of *The You Know* walked away with him, and some of *The You Know* crept after me. I watched him drive away, his red brake lights a warning. I didn't want *The You Know* getting in the car with me, so I threw it to the ground and stomped it. It wasn't dead, of course, because *The You Know* was fuelled by the Alleged Offender and his cadre, but it was at least miserable, bruised, and sputtering.

Me, I drove away without a backward glance.

small birds

KIM GOLDBERG

small birds, invisible
to distant eye, cry out at dusk
or is it just
the groan of fir limbs
rushed with wind, blown into
each other by forces of covert animation
beyond their control?
a cone drops
lands with soft thud on
forest duff   there is a moment
of stillness in which vectors
pause

anything is possible

and then a sylvan committee is struck
to determine why the cone
was not more firmly attached
and whether this pattern could

spread to other cones
causing a wide-scale cone drop and crisis
of confidence in forests overall
and are the invisible
birds at fault? their cries
(or errant wind) must be or diminished
so the innocent do not become
buried under fir needles and leaf mould
and bat shit, for it is the lofty cones
we care about here, in case
you've lost track
their vital seed will spawn
the next forest
birds come and go
like the wind

🔥

Notes

I wrote "small birds" on November 21, 2016, one week after dozens of major
Canadian authors signed an open letter to the University of British Columbia titled "Steven Galloway's Right to Due Process." Galloway, the former
chair of UBC's Creative Writing department, had been fired after an investigation into various complaints.

The letter sparked a long-running and highly visible discussion on
social media under the #ubcaccountable hashtag about rape culture at
post-secondary institutions and beyond. So overwhelming was the outrage
and criticism over this letter and its signatories that I found it hard to add
my voice without repeating what had already been said by hundreds of
others. This poem emerged from my struggle to find new language to
express my own astonishment and disappointment that so many of my
literary colleagues would sign such a letter, essentially repudiating sexual
assault complainants and survivors everywhere. I posted the poem on

social media at the time. But without a note adding context, readers took it to be simply a pleasant lyrical excursion into a forest. (The poet's eternal dilemma: to explain, or not explain.)

The other way I found to contribute something unique to the #ubcaccountable debate was to post running tallies on Facebook and Twitter identifying which signatories subsequently removed their names from the open letter, and which people subsequently added their names to it post-publication. The open letter, with its ever-changing list of signatories, was posted for all to see on the UBCAcountable website. I merely took stock of who left and who joined, and then posted the results on social media. The list of signatories ceased changing on January 3, 2017, at which point twenty-one of the original signatories had left the list, and twenty-nine new signatories had added their names, bringing the total number of signatories on the Open Letter to UBC up to ninety-two.

In response to my updates on the list of signatories, former Vancouver poet laureate Brad Cran likened my actions to "McCarthyism" and to the Stasi (East Germany's notorious secret police) in his Twitter postings.* The fact that I was simply reformatting content that had been publicly posted on the UBCAccountable website apparently escaped Cran's notice.

In January 2018, the seemingly dormant open letter and list of signatories came back to life after Concordia University in Montreal suspended two creative writing instructors amid allegations of sexual misconduct. In the following days, fourteen more signatories to the UBCAccountable open letter championing Galloway removed their names. And, bizarrely, four new people decided to add their names to the pro-Galloway letter.** The wave of #MeToo testimonials had been underway for three months at this point.

In March 2018, the UBCAccountable open letter in aid of Galloway was archived, effectively immortalizing it in cyberspace.

Citation

"small birds" first appeared in *Event*, Spring 2018.

🔥

Tweet from @bradcran: "@eleanecorden @roblucastaylor sorry then Rob. I'm offended by @KimPigSqash's naming list. It reeks of mccarthyism. It bothers me to my core" [Posted 11:35 am, 22 Nov 2016]

Tweet from @bradcran: "@KimPigSqash No not @kaspoitman! Good work Kim! "Schild und Schwert er Partei"" [Posted 11:50 pm, 26 Nov 2016]

🔥

Names removed from or added to the #UBCAccountable letter
as of January 19, 2018

NAMES REMOVED

1. Kathryn Kuitenbrouwer
2. Wayne Johnston
3. Jean Baird
4. George Murray
5. Carrie Snyder
6. Sheila Heti
7. Saleema Nawaz Webster
8. Camilla Gibb
9. Miriam Toews
10. Andrew Westoll
11. John K. Samson
12. Erik Rutherford
13. Christine Fellows
14. Carolyn Forde
15. Ryan Knighton
16. Noah Richler

NAMES ADDED

1. Andrew Fleming
2. Barbara Lambert
3. Shaughnessy Bishop-Stall
4. Elizabeth Abbott
5. Jeyn Roberts
6. Derek Mah
7. Jack Hodgins
8. David Cronenberg
9. C.C. Humphreys
10. Holly McNarland
11. Ross King
12. Ken McGoogan
13. Allan Stratton
14. Steven Hayward
15. J. Jill Robinson
16. Julie Salverson

17. Dave Bidini
18. Shandi Mitchell
19. Yann Martell
20. Alice Kuipers
21. Dede Crane

Since Jan. 12, 2018:
22. Lisa Moore
23. Karen Solie
24. Madeleine Thien
25. Michael Helm
26. Meryn Cadell
27. Lee Henderson
28. Sheri Benning
29. Jonathan Bennett
30. Rawi Hage
31. Adam Sol
32. Mitchell Parry
33. Jeanette Lynes
34. Sharon Thesen
35. Shaughnessy Bishop-Stall

17. Carmen Rodriguez
18. Stan Persky
19. Giles Blunt
20. Patrick Warner
21. Mitchell Parry
22. Greg Gatenby
23. Dennis E. Bolen
24. Michael Boughn
25. Brian Fawcett
26. Meryn Cadell
27. Joelene Heathcote
28. David Staines
29. David Mount

Since Jan. 12, 2018:
30. Sandra Martin
31. Laura Kipnis
32. Hal Wake
33. Terry Glavin

Corrections welcome if I have misrepresented anyone's status. —Kim Goldberg

Stars Upon Thars
The Sneetches and Other CanLit Stories

TANIS MacDONALD

In social media discussions following the #UBCAccountable letter, I read many good analyses of gender and power. But mainstream media coverage set off the insistent clanging I always hear whenever class plays a vital but undiscussed role in public discourse. Class is the social designation Canada hates to talk about but loves to invoke without explanation. I was surprised to read in articles summarizing the public discussion that CanLit was an agreed-upon and agreeable entity. Whose CanLit is that? Not mine. Class was the unspoken privilege invoked by the media's hyperbolic term "CanLit stars," but also by the elitist positioning of the #UBCAccountable letter in "calling out" a university, inferring that when "celebrity" authors talk, people— including lowly ink-stained hacks like university administrators, union reps, profs, and students who pay tuition to study these authors—ought to listen and obey if they know what side their bread is buttered on. That last phrase is my mother's, who would invoke what side my bread was buttered on not to remind me to keep my place, but rather to remind me from where my livelihood came, and to whom I owe my attention. I have given CanLit my attention as a scholar and as a poet for two decades, and with the full weight of those two decades and the doubled perspective *and* the approbation of my late mother who taught me to whom I owe my attention, I ask this: Exactly who is kidding whom here about class, privilege, and power?

Brian Bethune's article in *Maclean's*, dated November 23, 2016, was headlined "How the Steven Galloway Affair Became a CanLit Class War." Bethune was not the only journalist to report on the fallout from the letter in class terms that are as creaky as they are inaccurate. In the *Globe*, Marsha Lederman trotted out "the hallowed halls of CanLit," Peter Darbyshire in the *Vancouver Sun* spun "CanLit stars," and Simon Lewsen in *The Walrus* went for both "CanLit's luminaries" and "A-list." Bethune, not to be outdone, called the signatories of the #UBCAccountable letter "a glittering array of prominent writers." Why do these overdetermined class terms matter to the media coverage of #UBCAccountable, and why should writers and critics and students (as they exist separately and as they often exist concurrently in, as Simon Lewsen calls them, the "un-famous") care about this public dalliance with hyperbole? Why does this remind me so much of Dr. Seuss's Sneetches, those creatures who have green stars on their bellies and disdain the ones who do not have "stars upon thars"?

The casting of the original signatories of the #UBCAccountable letter as high status is a curious construction. The media's favourite metaphor of a spat between high-status "makers" and low-status "partakers" implies that Canadian writers (as an amorphous mass) occupy a tony artisan class who are served by a sweating and striving serfdom of students and profs, and any change in that dynamic would upset the righteous avuncular balance. The fact that many of those "serfs" are also writers—and that many of the writers are also profs—was all but dismissed by people like Stephen Marche, who tweeted on November 24, 2016: "An interesting point . . . is that everyone in the country who can actually write well is on Galloway's side." Beware of tweeters bearing the phrase "everyone in the country" and the expert-making word "actually." Was Marche, a novelist who did his doctorate in early modern drama, trying to separate himself from the sixteenth century and insert himself among the ranks of "CanLit stars" via this expression of "good writer" solidarity? If so, he would not be the only one. The original #UBCAccountable "array" would have been be a good deal less than glittering without the names of award winners Boyden, Thien, Atwood, and Martel; since Thien and Martel have removed their signatures, the list is not so impressive. It must be said that many of the #UBCAccountable writer-signers are pretty "un-famous" themselves, and I have to wonder how much of their motivation to sign was pure careerism, the impulse to align themselves with the righteous 'tude of those with good sales numbers. To list themselves alongside bestsellers, and so to become one of the literary Sneetches with "stars upon thars."

In Paul Fussell's shoot-from-the-hip analysis of social status, *Class*, he isolates the concept of "Prole Drift...the tendency in advanced industrialized societies for everything to become proletarianized" (172). A class analysis of the #UBCAccountable coverage suggests Upper-Class Drift, what I will call the tendency in an anxious cultural climate for creators to accept media-fuelled aristocratization. (Fussell does not ignore artists, but he designates them "X people" whose category separates them from class.) Upper-Class Drift is insidious, and the more phrases like "a glittering array of prominent writers" are repeated, the more they mask the dynamic at work in the #UBCAccountable letter that discredits young and emerging female writers and feminist professors of all ages and genders. This presumptive metaphor of a class war keeps the media from a gender analysis—or even a real class analysis—that would include many of those professors and all of those students in the category of "X people": creative makers who are also partakers.

Such an insistence on the "star class" was visually reinforced by the parallel poses of Chelsea Rooney and Sierra Skye Gemma in the photo that accompanies Marsha Lederman's *Globe* article "Under a Cloud." Both young female writers are shown huddled on adjoining sets of cracked concrete steps like the little match girls of CanLit. Why so Dickensian? Madeleine Thien's photo shows her in a green and lovely backyard, and Galloway's stock photo shows him in a jacket and tie. Why was it necessary, or even interesting, to imply class differences visually and so sharply in this article that purported to be about an employee's dispute with his employer? How then must we read the "class" of CanLit academics who signed the counter-letter, Galloway's scholarly colleagues, those who determine the cultural and political temperature in "the hallowed halls of CanLit"? Academics are almost always glossed as "elites," but this time the media struggled to cast the writers as knowing elites and the academics as outdated servants.

In her indispensable 2000 book *where we stand: class matters*, bell hooks identifies the panic that rises, especially in the lower middle class who are themselves only one job loss (or, I will add, one book failure) away from being poor, whenever discussions of class or status surface. The perceived danger of these conversations is that they introduce the possibility that we may see and be seen in ways that we would like to control, but cannot, or in hooks's words: "The neat binary categories of white and black or male and female are not there when it comes to class. How will they identify the enemy. How will they know who to fear and who to challenge" (hooks, 6).

Throughout *where we stand*, hooks asserts that these conversations are as vital as those that everyone in North America needs to have about race, and she links the history and construction of race in North America as almost always dependent on a dogged refusal to acknowledge class structures and possible solidarity between working peoples. She takes as her primary principle that we must crack open our resistance to talking about class in North America in order to reveal the fundamental ideologies that are used to manipulate so many of us, and even to police our own speech, so much so that we will perpetually resist the very solidarity that might empower us. So was class called up by the media as a dutiful spectre from the class systems of the Great Beyond—like Manservant Hecubus on *The Kids in the Hall*—to manufacture consent about who was powerful enough to fear and who was weak enough to challenge? Fussell's bumper-sticker-succinct aphorism that the middle class is "distinguishable more by its earnestness and psychic insecurity than by its middle income" (39) may explain some people's eagerness to sign the initial letter. To that end, we might reimagine Camilla Gibb's "Because I am still a woman" via its classed parallel: the nearly unsayable "Because I am still working class and desperate to be included." Sometimes being class-scared means pretending you know what you definitely do not and hoping no one calls you on it.

The narrative reinforced is that of the great unwashed pushing back against the deservedly glam: *The Day of the Locust* brought to CanLit. The hollowness of this rhetoric should be completely exposed by the economic realities of the writing life, most recently on display in Michael Redhill's tweet of the deposit slip showing that he had $411 in the bank before depositing the $100,000 cheque that he received as the winner of the 2017 Giller Prize. The popular fantasy that the literary life "glitters" for CanLit stars with their crystalline prose and sparkling wit pervades the media coverage of the #UBCaccountable letter. Hyperbolic or not, the metaphor of a literary class war perpetuates a false division that produced (and is still producing) the righteous rhetoric that writers "know" and that others (their readers, be they profs, students, or yes, other writers) cannot possibly access that specialized knowledge. This is pretentious enough in a writing workshop, and it makes no sense at all when the "specialized knowledge" in question is the content of confidential legal documents. What is trotted out as definitive is in fact derivative. The media that framed this letter and the resistance to it as a class war did so to suit a national imaginary that has long instrumentalized CanLit as a self-affirming conservative commodity.

Not everyone was fooled, and not everyone was eager to get a piece of this drifted stardom. Novelist Zoe Whittall's use of cautionary quotes skews the Drift in Marsha Lederman's *Globe* article of November 18, 2016: "There is a woman with no support and an entire community who does not believe her, and in this case, an entire group of 'Can Lit Stars' willing to disregard her in the name of holding a university accountable." Brit Bachmann extends the use of class irony even further in "It's Only Castles Burning," her December 5, 2016, editor's note in the online *Discorder* magazine. Bachmann strikes a note of wry but genuine despair when she parallels the deaths of many boomer heroes in 2016 to the death of liberal thought in North America, calling Atwood's decline as a feminist hero a sign of the Apocalypse.

Fussell's point that "taste" functions as code for class has a deep resonance in Canada. In fact, "taste" has been used by more than one literary critic in Canada to determine the parameters of CanLit worth. Invoking class outright would result in critics being decried as snobs, but using "taste" or "craft" as the special province of a coterie is a cultural deke, limited though they are as terms with which to describe individual pieces of work, let alone an entire national literature. The term "tastemaker" is so presumptuous I can't say it without convulsing. I am still deciding whether the convulsion is laughter or a desire to protect my vital organs. In 2012, Russell Smith used the term unironically, calling Michael Lista and Carmine Starnino "combative tastemakers," though he also called Lista "truculent" with "narrow and exclusive" taste. This fanboy non-debate between three white literary guys in cosmopolitan Canada who work prominently in the arts and culture industries and can't appear to decide which fella exactly like themselves represents them best is far outside the context of most people's reading practices and economic realities. It also smacks heavily of C. S. Lewis's definition of gluttony in Letter XVII of *The Screwtape Letters*: he defines gluttony not as the desire to consume mass amounts, but rather a querulous and attention-grabbing insistence on upholding (and forcing others to uphold) esoteric standards that are fussily hard to meet (Lewis, 86–87). The gluttony of Delicacy is in the uncharitable impulse to corral all the attention, all the time, all of the high standards; gluttony is exclusively self-concerned. Scarcity and class are necessarily linked, and the tautology that taste isn't taste unless it's refined by those who know is infuriatingly abroad in the world.

When you are of a certain class, it is easy to pretend that you live in a classless society: that you're beyond it and above it. But for others, it's equally impossible to pretend it doesn't exist. I'm a striving-class-raised cis-gendered white woman in the academy and in the Canadian literary community, and still adjusting to being firmly middle-class, so I know all about hiding in plain sight. Class and status in the media coverage of #UBCAccountable continue to signify in my ongoing work, beginning with my choice of publishers with whom I work, and proceeding through who I teach and how I advise students and young writers. As for the metaphor of a CanLit class war, at once so overused and so undertheorized, what a difference it could have made to public discussion if coverage of the #UBCAccountable letter had included an examination of this class metaphor rather than just perpetuating it. And what if, as part of that examination, we flipped the metaphor?

A sparkling panoply of the nation's hottest young authors teamed up with some of the nation's most respected and sharp-thinking academics, including many holders of prestigious SSHRC fellowships, Killam grants, and Canada Research Chairs, together representing centuries of experience in teaching and shaping the CanLit scene, to support victims of sexual violence and to remind a handful of misguided older authors of their debt to the upcoming glitterati of the new scene. It was a pleasure to see the best minds in the country and the brightest stars in a new creative universe working together in a labour of love: to shift CanLit conservatism—buoyed by two or three bestselling authors who seem rather out of touch—into low gear given their haste in signing a document demanding favouritism for one of their own.

Such rhetorical reversals, politically satisfying though they might be, are not meant to balance the violence of the original metaphor but rather to draw attention to the power differential between those who benefit from it and those who are ignored, discarded, or reduced by it.

In 2014, accepting her medal for Distinguished Contribution to American Letters from the National Book Foundation, Ursula K. Le Guin noted, "[P]rofit motive is often in conflict with the aims of art. We live in capitalism. Its power seems inescapable—so did the divine right of kings." The media's division of Canadian writers into aristocratic makers and serflike partakers does not advance discussion, but instead shows a marked social and cultural investment in conserving a capitalist status quo. In the Dr. Seuss story, the Sneetches discover that their stars can be removed and applied by a machine and, in the ensuing rush to trumpet the superiority of their differences, they lose track of who is who in the chaos. For the Sneetches, it means learning tolerance. In CanLit, who knows? Maybe we will learn to live without class-shaming. Perhaps we will see the fall of the CanLit divine right of kings. I wonder how we will talk then. I wonder how we will write.

How It Works

TANIS MacDONALD

*If our happiness depends on turning away from violence, our happiness
is violence.*

—Sara Ahmed

Not a rockstar, not
an up-and-comer,
neither mover nor

quaker, not a hot
commodity, not
this year's it girl.

I have written
a thousand polite
emails without

coughing up blood or that
book of the season,
so fresh, listable,

now. Know me? I've
taught so many
for so long

on the verge of
a nervous system
reboot, I have

resting teach face
in this testing
pitch place. I am not

your canon or firing
pin, not your elbow
patches, not your

mid-calf A-line
skirt. I'm not that kind
of churl, not

a scrappy little
fighter, not
a pistol, not feisty,

not spicy, not
doable
the way I know you

use doable.
My lack of fucks
stream

into your hard
drive, circumnavigate
your circle (jerk),

your goingaround
now comingaround.
I know you could not

see me when you
assigned me to the kill
floor, but I worked

my way up, staining
the aprons of stages,
punching the doomsday

clock like I was born
to break time into
a unionized wage.

My spilled ink floats
beneath your
radar. Tell me again

how it works.

But I Still Like

GWEN BENAWAY

can lit is a mythology

    just like this country
    it gets hard off

        apathy.

    famous feminist Canadian writers
        argue that sexual assault is just
            a lack of dating etiquette
      our legendary writers
        moonlight as rape apologists

    but this is a safe country
        for the bodies marked neutral, natural and sovereign

      leave that fact
      off the brochure

'cause can lit

          is about landscape
          surviving winter
          gardening
          clever wordplay

while the dispossessed bodies disappear
from highways leading

          to good intentions
          and genocide

but the merciful white cis folk
    will save us all with their feminist manifestos
        retweet the protest anthem
            "buy diverse literature"
because consumption is something
        Canadians respect.

    they make their good tokens into offerings

    the sweet fetish of the hour
        and the promise
            of a better award season.

at least rapists get exposed
    a decade later
        and the conversation is changing, y'all

while the dead are still dead
    and the missing still miss
        the way home.

can lit is cis lit
regardless the colour
or delineation
though it's acceptable to question gender
as long as you don't embody it
in a sincere way
or ask others
to see you as they see themselves.

except I had the "surgery"
and my tell all memoir poetry collection
will win the GG*

*I'm joking because transsexuals don't win awards because that would
mean our bodies have value and for an object to have worth, it first has to
exist in the mind of the appraiser and in order to imagine the wilderness
they imagine Canada to be, can lit has to erase everyone that isn't empty
in order to make themselves something and that's why a transsexual will
never win an award because we are not wild enough nor empty enough
and therefore we don't exist along with everyone else who isn't white or
can't act convincingly like whiteness because the artifact and the value
and the body and the literary
is to become so empty
they can fill you with themselves

and once we have diverse juries and diverse writers and diverse readers
and diverse books*
*all of whom are mostly cis
can lit will be fixed
refused

and we will become the diverse empty

                    they pour their mythological self into

      and from us will emerge

                        the same old new nothing.

#CanLit at the Crossroads
Violence Is Nothing New; How We Deal with It Might Be

LUCIA LORENZI

"Today's CanLit is all about next-level polarization," wrote Marsha Lederman in a February 2018 piece in the *Globe and Mail*, "a bigger-than-the-Gillers grudge match that has blown up into an all-out war—with divisions largely, but not always, along generational lines. It would make a great novel (if it isn't already being written—and it probably is)." Lederman's article, which offered an update regarding the so-called "civil war" that has been unfolding in very public-facing ways since November 2016, provided a sort of general update for readers who may have followed events such as the firing of UBC professor Steven Galloway and the discussions around cultural appropriation that emerged as a result of former *Write* magazine editor Hal Niedzviecki's suggestion of the creation of an "appropriation prize."

Within the communities of CanLit—those whose struggles are being made extremely public, particularly on platforms such as Twitter—hearts are heavy, nerves frayed: understandably so. What strikes me as strange within much of the larger public discourse, however, and what seems entirely counter to actually confronting the situation at hand, is the suggestion (by some) that this is a grand ideological and generational rift of contemporary Canadian literature, and that if only we could hearken back to the days of cozy literary compatriotism, we might be able to heal the wounds caused by the events of the past year or two, particularly with regards to the UBCAccountable letter and the aftermath of Steven Galloway's firing from the UBC Creative Writing department.

For those who may be less familiar with Canadian literature as a literary community, as a scholarly discipline, and as a national cultural institution (intertwined as these all are, given the tight-knit nature of Canadian literary production and criticism), I can understand why this might seem like a shocking turn of events. After all, literature is so embedded in our collective Canadian consciousness that since 1979, our national broadcasting company has sponsored a prestigious writing competition, one that, as described by the CBC itself, allows writers to potentially "become a star overnight," and suggests that their "phone[s] will be ringing off the hook" (*CBC Books*, n.p.). Moreover, since 2002, the CBC has also hosted Canada Reads, a "battle of the books" in which five celebrities champion five different books during a week-long, publicly broadcast television and radio event that results in the selection of one book that all of Canada should read. This is, all told, a seemingly unique national pastime, and one not without both significant economic and cultural impact. As UBC English professor Laura Moss notes in a 2004 editorial in *Canadian Literature*, the inaugural competition was so terrifically popular that the winning novel, Michael Ondaatje's *In the Skin of the Lion*, "sold approximately eighty thousand copies more in 2002 than in 2001" (p. 6). However, as Moss also points out, her unease about events such as Canada Reads lies precisely in the sort of collective-yet-entirely-depoliticized national spirit it attempts to promote: "Canada Reads has become a new instrument of culture formation. It is intent on drawing Canadians together by creating a shared cultural background. The winning titles reinforce certain popular notions of Canadianness" (p. 7). In other words, at least part of the public project of Canadian literature, much like the idea of Canada itself, has been to promote a narrative that runs counter to the existing rifts and violent histories within itself.

Twelve years after Moss published this editorial, it is safe to say that the bizarre and mutually reinforcing relationship between Canada and its national literature, at least in its popular and public image, has reached a fever pitch. Writers like Margaret Atwood and Joseph Boyden have become outspoken critics and prominent national voices in conversations around climate change, political freedoms, and Canada's ongoing legacy of colonialism. To say that Canadian authors have merely adopted the roles of public intellectuals, cultural ambassadors, or social critics would be an understatement; in many cases, their voices and names have actually eclipsed those of other scholars, critics, and intellectuals. In an article for national magazine *The Walrus* entitled "The CanLit Firestorm," Simon Lewsen suggests that "[a]long with David Suzuki and the NDP, CanLit was the moral conscience of the nation. That's not to say it was didactic... but just that people wrote with a sense of ethical purpose, and readers appreciated their commitment." This sense of morals or ethics, Lewsen argues, translated into serious cultural power for several Canadian writers, who, whether they wanted it or not, became "CanLit... heroes—powerful, established heroes, whose reigns lasted decades."

In the early days after the publication of the UBCAccountable website and letter, Margaret Atwood defended herself against the "bullies" and "keyboard warriors" who were inflicting "burn wounds" and "noose marks" on the signatories of the letter, and *Briarpatch Magazine* removed Joseph Boyden as one of the judges of their Writing in the Margins literary contest because of his involvement with the letter. Criticism and consequences came from within the CanLit community itself: it's hardly what most would have expected, which might explain the shock and awe of media who are still attempting to understand precisely what is going on. Even Lewsen suggested that "[s]uddenly, CanLit's inner circle is looking less like moral trailblazers and more like an establishment—an institution with its own internal values and interests to defend."

Of course, the truth is that CanLit has *always* been an institution with its own internal values and interests to defend, and while Lewsen is correct in suggesting that the "once quiet precincts of CanLit are suddenly more rancorous than they've been in decades," CanLit was never a "community that once seemed harmonious," particularly for those who have been either pre-emptively or retroactively excluded, especially when they have actively pushed back against the CanLit establishment. Although I am a Canadianist by training, I do not claim to have a comprehensive view of Canadian literary history and each instance of fissure and fracture within its ranks. What I can say, however, is that a literary tradition that includes the Confederation Poets as part of its origin story—a group of white men and a woman or two, including former deputy superintendent of the Department of Indian Affairs Duncan Campbell Scott, who sought to "get rid of the Indian problem"—is necessarily going to have to constantly fight with its past and ongoing colonial, patriarchal, and white-supremacist histories. A literary tradition that has been Anglocentric in nature and has excluded Québécois literature from its canon must confront its past and ongoing francophobia. A literary history that has either dismissed Indigenous literatures written in Canada, or appropriated them without any recognition of or respect for Indigenous literary and cultural sovereignty, must confront its past and ongoing colonialism. A literary history that includes significant backlash against those who organized the 1994 Writing Thru Race conference, some events at which were open only to self-identified writers of colour—some called it a "a nasty serving of cultural apartheid"—must confront its past and ongoing white supremacy. A literary history that has traditionally been dominated by men (see the work of Canadian Women in the Literary Arts for their vital work in this area) must confront its past and ongoing patriarchy. A literary history that includes the unlawful seizure of queer literature at the Canadian borders, and the recent attempts to censor and rescind a Governor General's Award–winning text—Raziel Reid's *When Everything Looks Like the Movies*—for its explicit content must confront its past and ongoing homophobia and transphobia. A literary history that still fails to centre disabled writers must confront its past and ongoing ableism, as has been called for by Dorothy Palmer, Bronwyn Berg, and Jane Eaton Hamilton, who founded CripCanLit as a means of recentring disabled writers.

And so, to suggest that CanLit has, as Lewsen has argued, "[operated] under a broadly progressive consensus" is to deny that the tensions of the past year and a half or so reflect a much broader history of oppression, or, as Vancouver poet and scholar Ryan Fitzpatrick has phrased it, that "what gets called CanLit is historically a site of struggle." To suggest that Canadian literature is monolithic as a genre, that it ought to encompass a certain canon of texts, or indeed, that its community of writers, critics, and scholars have historically achieved "consensus" of any kind is revisionist history at best. At worst, it perpetuates the kinds of ideological formations of community that make it difficult, if not impossible, for oppressed people to speak up against those who wield power.

CanLit, we might then say, is a kind of "imagined community," to borrow the term coined by political scientist and historian Benedict Anderson. In 1983, Anderson theorized the nation as a social construction held up in large part by the idea that while we might never meet most of our fellow country-persons (or writers, scholars, and critics), we imagine a sort of "communion" between them and ourselves: we project shared interests, mutual values, and a common history, even if all or none of these exist. Perhaps the most pointed and valuable part of Anderson's notion of "imagined community" is the idea that "regardless of the actual inequality and exploitation that may prevail in each, the nation is always conceived as a deep, horizontal comradeship. Ultimately it is this fraternity that makes it possible, over the past two centuries, for so many millions of people, not so much to kill, as willingly to die for such limited imaginings" (7). Anderson is referring here largely to the context of war, but his argument nevertheless raises questions about similar dynamics within the imagined community that is CanLit: *What are the actual inequalities and exploitations that prevail within it? How is this "deep, horizontal comradeship" constructed and upheld, and by whom? How far are we willing—or forced—to go in order to defend it or suffer for it?*

With regards specifically to Steven Galloway's firing, as well as the revelations of abuses in the Creative Writing department at Concordia, we have to acknowledge the dynamics of power that lie within the institutional and educational environments of literary study and instruction. In a field such as creative writing, when professors' roles as mentors not only include instruction but also function as gateways to literary careers, the power wielded by instructors is immense, as is the damage caused when this

relationship is exploited or violated. In "Stories Like Passwords," publi
in the *Hairpin* in 2014, Emma Healey describes how this power operates,
particularly in situations where there is harassment and assault:

> The men in stories like this always have just enough power, in their
> little worlds and in ours, that to confront them would be to court an
> ordeal, to invite others to question our own memories and motives.
> It's always more trouble than it's worth. If you don't have hard proof,
> if you don't have a police report, then what do you have? Only what
> you remember. Only what you felt.

Safe to say that the repercussions—both personal and professional—of
reporting any sort of misconduct or harassment (be it the theft of a student's
work or an assault perpetrated against the student) have to be carefully
weighed alongside the realities of the systems we currently operate within.
It takes immense courage to come forward with a complaint, because as
those who have reported various forms of misconduct, violence, and oppression know all too well, there are truly few benefits to doing so (despite the
claims that there is a pot of gold at the end of the survivor-rainbow, which
I can certainly attest to being nothing but a falsehood perpetuated by vic-
tim-blamers). Rather, there are likely more consequences: the loss of
friends, the loss of a potential career, the loss of income, the loss of time, the
loss of sleep, the loss of trust. More often than not, I suspect, victims do not
come forward precisely because they have been conditioned to worry about
the health and well-being of "the community" over and above their own. *Don't
cause a fuss. Don't disturb the peace. It's for the greater good.*

While we have a tendency to individualize the problem of violence and
misconduct within our communities—"bad apples" or "lone wolves," depend-
ing on the case—we know, too, that there are systems of power that actively
uphold and defend those who enact harm. I don't mean to suggest this is
always deliberate. I doubt that all the signatories of the UBCAccountable
letter are part of some scheming cabal of CanLit literati who seek to destroy
anyone who speaks ill of them or deigns to file a complaint against one of

their own. (They're not.) Rather, the system—the entire system—is built to accommodate those who do harm, and it is upheld by much more than a few staunch defenders or unwitting apologists.

This is, therefore, decidedly *not* new, and certainly not limited to UBC or Concordia or even the field of creative writing. These power dynamics and forms of institutional support predate those currently accused of sexual assault and harassment. After all, Healey's piece was published in 2014, a full year before the first rumblings were stirred about the Galloway case, as was CWILA's project "Love, Anonymous," which, in the wake of the Ghomeshi trial, offered a series of stories about various experiences of assault and abuse within Canadian literary communities. It is true that the Galloway case has emerged as a distinct flashpoint in the national conversation on institutional policy and procedure, sexual misconduct, and sexual violence, and it is also true that it very publicly centres these issues in the literary community like perhaps never before. But it is not new, has never been new, will never be new: it is embedded in our society, of which CanLit is (despite the utopian yearnings of writers' unique enlightenment) certainly a part.

If we can acknowledge that CanLit as both an abstract construct and as a concrete community of people has always been marred and complicated by power and violence, then we are asked to face a much broader and more frightening reality, which is that, regardless of the outcome of any particular grievance, there are serious issues to be faced within the community. As much as I agree wholeheartedly that university processes of handling such cases are inherently flawed (insofar as they work to protect the institutions, not the faculty, students, or staff), and that systemic change must be made in order to give due process and fair treatment to both complainants and respondents, we cannot rely on universities and the police alone to somehow solve the problem of violence and abuses of power.

A lack of evidence as considered by universities and the law does not mean that we are absolved of having to consider these matters within our own circles. With the gross abuses of many universities and police forces — see what happened in Val-d'Or, where dozens of Indigenous women's cases of abuse by Sûreté du Québec police officers were dismissed—we also need to divest ourselves of the colonial power of these systems, because they are and will continue to be stacked against those who are the most vulnerable. I am not suggesting we completely abandon the system of reporting complaints to universities, or that we discourage survivors from wanting to engage with these institutional processes. As a survivor of sexual assault at UBC, and as a member of the expert panel tasked with making recommendations about best practices for UBC's standalone sexual assault policy, I have spent years railing against the injustices of the system. I understand the frustration so profoundly. I do, but so long as these institutions stand, it is imperative that we demand an ongoing commitment to supports for survivors.

In addition to advocating for institutional change that treats both parties fairly, I am also suggesting that CanLit as a community consider its own responsibilities, duties, and accountabilities toward each other: the responsibility not to abuse positions of power; the duty to recognize our privileges; the accountability to all members of a community, especially those who are most vulnerable.

We do this not by calling for a healing or ceasefire within our community, or by ignoring the elephant in the room: that now, as of the spring of 2018, many women have come forward with stories about assault and harassment at the hands of prominent Canadian writers, and that there are yet more such stories circulating within the community.

Having revisited this piece nearly a year and a half after first writing it, my original concerns about how violence in our communities is portrayed still stands. Much mainstream media coverage has yet to move past the facile analyses of historical dissent and to frame it to readers in a way that articulates the ongoing resistance of marginalized people within CanLit in all of its social and institutional iterations. So, too, does my concern about what is lost in so many of our conversations: those who have suffered, those who are continuing to suffer, and those who will suffer if we do not change how we deal with the myriad violences that are perpetrated within what we call CanLit.

Those who have come forward about abuse, more than anyone, have gotten lost in this whole mess, particularly the woman we only know as the Main Complainant in the Galloway case. She, more than anyone, deserves to be more than an anecdote in a story about how a literary community waged a "civil war," deserves to be heard over our din of self-congratulation and self-defence, rationalization and rage, deserves to be more than an example of how institutions fail miserably when it comes to sexual assault allegations, deserves to be more than a blip in Canadian literary history.

Part Two:
REFUSE

The first section of this book, on refusal, thinks about the moment of rupture when, in the words of Jacques Rancière, "what was only audible as noise comes to be heard as speech." It archives some of those initial responses and the way in which they constituted a turning away. But a turning away into what?

The second sense of "refuse" at play in *Refuse: CanLit in Ruins* is the noun: trash, junk, detritus. The language of garbage has been at play from some of the earliest interventions into the current CanLit crises, most notably in Jen Sookfong Lee's spring 2017 "Open Letters and Closed Doors: How the Steven Galloway Open Letter Dumpster Fire Forced Me to Acknowledge the Racism and Entitlement at the Heart of CanLit" and, in September of the same year, Alicia Elliott's "CanLit Is a Raging Dumpster Fire," a revised version of which opens this section. The language of the dumpster and the trash can have been a powerful litany, an insistence on refusing by renaming what has always been structured by silences and exclusions.

It is a significant political statement to declare a celebrated national literary culture "trash," to say that it is, or deserves to be, on fire, tossed in a dumpster, and burned to ashes. Focusing on the dumpster fire, like the injunction to stay with the trouble we discussed in the introduction, is a call not to move through the crisis of the moment into a hasty attempt at reconciliation or recovery. It stops us from cheerily plastering over the troubles in a desire to return to the false image of consensus that has so long characterized media accounts of CanLit. If we think of the recent events in CanLit as a rupture event, we might think of the garbage as what that rupture reveals: a national literature that, as part of a larger colonial project, was built on a foundation of injustices, including settler colonialism, anti-Blackness, and ableism. As Kai Cheng Thom writes in "refuse: a trans girl writer's story," "for fuck's sake the whole thing / is a settler colonial project / that is designed to gobble up / anything that it deems / powerful or precious."

The work done in this section is that of naming CanLit as always-already trash by identifying the kinds of garbage that exist within it. For Alicia Elliott, that work involves naming the racism, neocolonialism, and myriad forms of entitlement that saturate CanLit. The 2017 "Appropriation Prize" controversy is a case in point: as Elliott points out, issues about the appropriation of Indigenous stories by non-Native writers were raised by Anishinaabekwe writer Lenore Keeshig in the 1980s. Elliott's article makes clear that racism in CanLit is nothing new either: Rinaldo Walcott's announcement at a 2017 conference that he was "quitting CanLit" is connected here to his extensive work on the erasure of Black life from CanLit history.

Decades ago, attempts to do anti-racist work in CanLit were met by significant opposition. In the early 1990s, Timothy Findley and Alberto Manguel, among others, opposed attempts to bring appropriation-of-voice policy to the Canada Council.[1] In response to criticism that he appropriated Indigenous stories, W. P. Kinsella said repeatedly that because he was a writer, he was entitled to write about Indigenous people if he wanted to. The Writing Thru Race conference of 1994, controversial (for some white writers) because it was organized by a coalition of BIPOC writers and only people of colour and Indigenous people could participate in its daytime sessions, focused significant attention on racism, neocolonialism, and the exclusion of minority voices in CanLit, and touched off debates about racism and appropriation across Canada. Statements in favour of cultural appropriation were met with the eloquent arguments of Larissa Lai, Roy Miki, Daniel David Moses, Lillian Allen, Maria Campbell, Dionne Brand, and Lee Maracle—among many others—as they called CanLit, and Canada, to account for its colonialism and racism. Knowing these histories is pivotal to understanding the dangers of naming the dumpster fires as a recent phenomenon. To do so implies that an earlier version of CanLit, one in which the hegemony of whiteness was taken for granted by the authors and critics who dominated the field, was not itself a thing worth refusing.

Sonnet L'Abbé is also grappling with history and with literary inheritance, as she works with and against what is one of the most overdetermined traditional literary forms. The sonnet carries associations with the thirteenth-century Italian poet Petrarch, with William Shakespeare, and with notions of form tension and resolution. L'Abbé's poems do not look like sonnets, but if you listen carefully you can find the original trace material. These poems, which engage Shakespeare's sonnets, work to both reterritorialize and, at the same time, silently listen. There is a rich literary history of "writing back" to dominant and hegemonic traditions, as well as questioning how writing from margin to so-called centre works to destabilize the centre. Drawing from philosophical traditions and lyrical tactics such as those of Audre Lorde, Sara Ahmed, Dionne Brand, Gloria Anzaldua, and M. NourbeSe Philip, these sonnets centralize mixed-race and Black women's thinking and engagement with history in the present. In moving Shakespeare's language from the centre, L'Abbe's poems demonstrate how much more there is to hear without trying to speak over or for others.

The question of the genres in which we speak and name ourselves in relation with the world is also central to Marie Carrière's contribution. Writing from the perspective of the university and the study of Canadian literature, she thinks through the work of self-situation and acknowledgements of power in relation to a feminist ethics of care. Naming ourselves, our positions in relation to power, can be a rich starting point, but also an insufficient one. Recognizing insufficiency and limitations without moving to change the situation could, she suggests, lead to another kind of dumpster politics.

In "refuse: a trans girl writer's story," Kai Cheng Thom addresses some of the ways in which "CanLit" functions as metonym for the settler-colonial project of nation-building. Moving across the cis, heteronormative, racialized, and gentrified spaces of major urban centres, Thom articulates the multiple ways the nation disavows so many bodies and experiences. Thom bases her critique in historical fact, citing the scores of workers from China who built the Canadian Pacific Railway, endured first the Head Tax and then the Chinese Exclusion Act, and still are underrepresented in the nation. Noting that she "wasn't a word in CanLit's vocabulary" either, Thom demands that readers recognize the detrimental effects of a homogenous national image. Yet, working in a tradition of rememoration and creation, Thom honours those who have been treated as the trash of the nation. Here, "refuse" becomes possibility, fertile with the wildness of otherwise.

There is another kind of call for justice at work in Dorothy Ellen Palmer's essay, one that builds on her writing on Facebook, Twitter, and her blog, which has focused on what due process means and on the labour issues—including Steven Galloway's own rights to a grievance process—that the UBCAccountable open letter did not acknowledge. In this essay, Palmer connects disability activism in CanLit to a relatively unexamined problem with Joseph Boyden's identity claims: the question of adoption.

The hierarchical structures of literary culture are also central to writer and professor Natalee Caple's interview with writer Nikki Reimer. Reimer recalls a gathering of Vancouver writers who met regularly to talk about literature and social justice. Most of the members of the group were women; all were writers at various stages of their careers. Its non-hierarchical structure recalls, for Reimer, the concept of the rhizome as structure of connection that offers an alternative to traditional structures of power and influence. Located in Vancouver, the eventual site of the Kootenay School of Writing, the Western Front, and other groups organized around long-standing critiques of power vis-à-vis urban gentrification and dislocation, Reimer gestures to the ways in which many urban centres have deep histories of cultural resistance and community-making. The conversation moves from the specificity of Vancouver to reference key events, such as Hal Niedzviecki's inflammatory editorial "Winning the Appropriation Prize" in the Writer's Union of Canada publication *Write*, as well as the function of certain kinds of literary celebrity in reifying gatekeeping in literary production.

It certainly would be impossible to name CanLit as an always-already dumpster fire without naming and thinking through the problem of literary celebrity. And there is no doubt that Margaret Atwood's celebrity status as a writer makes her one of the most recognizable faces of CanLit in the world. To some, Margaret Atwood *is* CanLit. Her actions anywhere in the public sphere attract media attention and, as Lorraine York has shown in her own scholarship on Atwood, Atwood herself is very aware of the power of her celebrity persona, and the success of the literary industry on which it depends. Atwood's prominence is complex for subsequent generations of writers in Canada. On the one hand, she has been seen as a role model, especially for feminist writers. On the other, her insistence during the UBCAccountable controversy on centring her perspective and minimizing other approaches to the problems involved has done much to exacerbate tensions stemming from the UBCAccountable controversy and the structure of CanLit itself. In her contribution, York, one of the leading scholars of Atwood's work, thinks about the ethics of academic cultural capital and how it can work to either shore up or, alternately, critique and thus decentre the power of literary celebrity.

The final piece in this section is a powerful tying-together of the many forces that constitute the dumpster fire as it extends beyond CanLit into Canadian culture, society, and politics writ large. The title of Chelsea Vowel's poem "No Appeal" can be read in multiple ways. On the one hand, it is a direct response to the news of March 7, 2018, when Saskatchewan's Assistant Deputy Attorney General Anthony Gerein announced that there was "no basis" for appealing the verdict in the Gerald Stanley trial. Stanley had been charged with second-degree murder after fatally shooting Colten Boushie, a twenty-two-year-old from the Red Pheasant Cree Nation. The refusal of an appeal was based on the decision that no errors had been made during the trial; critics responded that the law itself is at fault. Stanley had been acquitted by an all-white jury, making it clear that the Canadian legal system—with its colonial roots—is designed to criminalize rather than defend Indigenous people. As Nehiyaw policy analyst and writer Emily Riddle, and Cree-Métis-Saulteaux writer, editor, and academic Lindsay Nixon have written, the Stanley verdict gives lie to the national project of "reconciliation": "Boushie's death points to an irony, hypocrisy, and superficiality of reconciliation, because the Canadian state is complicit in Boushie's death."[2] At the same time, "no appeal" refers to the perspective of many Indigenous people on CanLit as a national project that is happy to capitalize on their stories while refusing to model accountability to their communities. In this poem, Vowel draws powerful links between the state's complicity in the death of Indigenous youth and other ways in which Canada extracts and exploits Indigenous history and culture, including CanLit's celebration of cultural appropriation in the guise of a shared national identity.

Together, the contributions in this section work to stay with the trouble by naming the trash, the junk, the detritus that have long operated within CanLit as an industry and a cultural formation. They refuse the imperative— often implied—to move on, to get over it, to focus on the future. In unearthing the garbage of the past and present, they provide us with the vocabulary to name how we got to the dumpster fire, and to see how the dumpster fire has always been burning.

CanLit Is a Raging Dumpster Fire

ALICIA ELLIOTT

We've all said it, heard it, or, more than likely, done both at some point since November 2016. In fact, it would seem that dissatisfaction with the state of CanLit, strangely enough, is the current state of CanLit. One has to wonder: what is it about CanLit that makes people consider it a "dumpster fire"? Why are writers suddenly eagerly anticipating its fiery death? What are they hoping to build from the ashes?

It's not hard to point to one moment that definitively cracked the literary community in half: the November 14, 2016, UBCAccountable letter. That was a demand by over eighty prominent Canadian writers, publishers, literary agents, and artists for an independent inquiry into the process by which UBC fired former Creative Writing head Steven Galloway.[1] While many of the writers initially signed the UBCAccountable letter before any clear information about the allegations against Galloway was available, once it was confirmed by numerous sources that those allegations did involve sexual harassment and sexual assault, only a handful of writers removed their names. Apparently, this illustrious group had chosen their figurative hill to die on: the reputation of a critically acclaimed peer accused of committing sexual violence against one of his students.

As Kai Cheng Thom points out in her brilliant, searing essay "Sometimes Women Have to Make Hard Choices to Be Writers,"[2] powerful older men so often use their prestige to commit sexual violence against younger women that it's almost considered a rite of passage in the industry. Many women have experienced this trauma themselves at the hands of mentors and professors—and yet, strangely, still don't stop it from happening to others. Thom suggests this may be because, once a woman has established herself in CanLit, it is too painful and difficult to confront "the possibility that the same establishment that made her prosperous and proud is built on the exploitation of her sisters."

In her deeply personal essay "Open Letters and Closed Doors: How the Steven Galloway Open Letter Dumpster Fire Forced Me to Acknowledge the Racism and Entitlement at the Heart of CanLit," Jen Sookfong Lee describes feeling pain that closely parallels precisely what Thom describes.[3] She explains that, prior to the UBCAccountable open letter, the general consensus was that CanLit was left-leaning and progressive. Although she herself had experienced racism within the industry, she'd been denying the extent of this racism, especially to herself. After the Galloway controversy erupted, Sookfong Lee could no longer hold on to these illusions, and had to admit that having them in the first place only served to uphold the racism that so often hurt her. "I had to finally admit that I had been working in an industry that had never held a space open for me," she writes. Her own experience of CanLit "is not the CanLit experience I want for new writers."

While a lot of this anger has crystallized in the aftermath of the UBCAccountable open letter, the anger is ultimately part of something deeper—something that has been simmering beneath polite Canadian smiles for a very long time. It's bubbled over at key moments. For example, in 1989, when Anishinaabe poet Lenore Keeshig took non-Native writers to task for appropriating Native stories and voices.[4] Perhaps predictably, non-Native writers did not stop. They took Keeshig's request as censorship. Nearly thirty years later, in May 2017, the "Appropriation Prize" scandal broke: starting with Hal Niedzviecki suggesting in his introduction to the first all-Indigenous issue of *Write* magazine that white writers should try to "win the appropriation prize" in order to make their stories more interesting—and ending with some of the most well-connected, powerful white writers, editors, and columnists in Canada pledging money to literally start such a prize one night on Twitter. The exact same arguments used against Keeshig and other Black writers, Indigenous writers, and writers of colour in 1989 were trotted out in 2017, as if no time had passed at all.

We could also look at 1997, when Rinaldo Walcott published the landmark book *Black Like Who? Writing Black Canada*. This book described Canada's, and CanLit's, continual erasure of Black people from its history, as well as its tendency to view Black men as criminals. Twenty years later, seeing little progress, Walcott decided to quit CanLit, saying, "CanLit fails to transform because it refuses to take seriously that Black literary expression and thus Black life is foundational to it. CanLit still appears surprised every single time by the appearance of Black literary expression and Black life."[5]

How is CanLit continually making the same mistakes? Or, to put it more frankly, how do the writers, editors, publishers, and agents that make up CanLit live through those mistakes, hear them pointed out, do nothing to address them, then still somehow manage to tell themselves that CanLit is diverse and progressive? And why are we suddenly—finally—willing to actually see these mistakes now?

Before I go any further I should, perhaps, mention that I'm a Haudenosaunee woman and, therefore, have never felt any particular fondness for or identification with Canadian nationalism. It's quite difficult to feel nostalgic for the country that has been trying to systematically destroy my nation since before it was considered a proper nation itself. That said, this lack of patriotism does permit me a very necessary perspective; after all, if I'm not attached to Canada's national identity, I have no stake in maintaining it, and I feel no pain dismantling it.

You may see where I'm going with this and you may already be resisting. Wait. Bear with me. I believe this sudden anger at CanLit is the inevitable result of Canada's own national identity crumbling. When you think about it, it's really not that far-fetched. One could very easily go through this entire essay, swap the word *CanLit* for *Canada*, and it would still, for the most part, make perfect sense. What words have traditionally been employed to describe CanLit? *Polite. Liberal. Progressive. Welcoming.* Aren't these the exact words consistently used to describe Canada? And if CanLit's really none of these things, can we honestly believe that Canada is?

As Jian Ghomeshi's recent sexual assault trial showed, rape culture is built into the Canadian justice system.[6] What's more, this past February, *Globe and Mail* reporter Robyn Doolittle revealed in an extensive investigation that rape culture is also built into policing: Canadian police dismiss one in five sexual assault claims as "unfounded" before they can even go to trial.[7] Given this context, is it really surprising that so many powerful members of CanLit came forward to defend Steven Galloway, bandying about the word "unsubstantiated"—a close synonym for "unfounded"—in their open letter, as though it were incontestable truth?

In August 2017, Canadians spent an entire week debating whether Sir John A. MacDonald should be criticized by "today's standards."[8] MacDonald, the first prime minister of Canada, was also the genocidal leader behind creating residential schools, starving Indigenous people into signing away their land, outlawing our ceremonies, murdering Metis leader Louis Riel, and publicly executing Cree warriors in the largest mass execution in Canadian history—which he forced their families to watch. If Canadians refuse to listen to our perspectives on a man who actively killed our ancestors, stole their children, and outlawed our culture, is it any surprise they don't listen to our perspectives on non-Native writers appropriating that culture?

Canada continues to pride itself on, essentially, not being as bad as America—more polite, more tolerant. Yet the violent anti-Black racism that set in motion the Black Lives Matter movement is just as strong here. Black men like Pierre Coriolan, Abdirahman Abdi, and Andrew Loku continue to be killed by police officers who do not value their humanity. The lack of consequences for the officers who killed these men only reinforces and legitimizes this dehumanization. On top of that, racist carding policies that specifically target Black men, presuming them to be inherently criminal, continue. When Canadian institutions devalue and dehumanize Black

Canadian lives, can we really be surprised that CanLit devalues and marginalizes Black Canadian literature?

A national literature's job is to both define and uphold the nation. But what if that nation's foundational beliefs about itself are, well, lies? What's left for those who are creating national literature but to feel alienated, lost, hurt? Maybe, for those who still very much want to feel proud to be Canadian, it's simply easier to call CanLit a dumpster fire. That way, you don't have to call Canada itself a dumpster fire. You don't have to acknowledge how accepting and perpetuating Canada's national myths of politeness, acceptance, and multiculturalism necessarily erase any evidence to the contrary. You also don't have to acknowledge the existence of Canada's systemic discrimination—or how your silence on that discrimination may be making you complicit in upholding it.

It's complicated to love a country that still actively hurts so many of the people who live within it. Do you let your love make you blind, do you stop loving the country entirely, or do you acknowledge its imperfections, shrug, and try to love it anyway?

It doesn't have to be that simple. All of us as writers know the blessing and curse that is constructive criticism. Though we can objectively recognize that it ultimately makes our work better, when we're hearing that constructive criticism, it hurts. Sometimes for days, weeks, months, years. But eventually, we all sit down, assess the criticism, and do the work to fix the problems.

Currently, we're collectively mourning the loss of a CanLit—and a Canada—that was always an idea instead of a lived reality. It's fine to mourn, of course. It's natural. But we can't just stand around and complain about the dumpster fire in front of us forever. Eventually we have to grab some fucking fire extinguishers and put that fire out. In other words, we have to sit down, assess the criticism, and do the work to fix the problems.

We don't need to wait for stubborn, lagging institutions to change. We never have. We can make change ourselves, now. In fact, we are. So many amazing people are stepping forward and speaking out, or quietly writing revolutions. Take that momentum and build on it. Write the books you've always wanted to read. Encourage others to write the books you've always wanted to read. Celebrate those books. Mentor young writers. Become the support you wish you'd had. Put your ego aside and listen to the constructive criticism you need to hear. Learn from that criticism. Give both CanLit and Canada no choice but to become better.

Okay, enough talk. Are you ready? We've got a lot of work to do.

Sonnet's Shakespeare

SONNET L'ABBÉ

CXII

Your long, overbearing disputation of my point is so manly. Do you try hard for the impression of a filibustering lawyer whose prolix speech strives to lull its gathered listeners into capitulation? Or do you paternally bestow a lump of wisdom upon my brown forehead? What do you care if the W.H.O. calls me when a pestilential terror of ills imperils a country? Or if I am the number one deprogrammer of enemy backdoors? My knowledge need not obstruct your discussion of the shallow clichés you heard somewhere. Men like you, all over the world, understand that I must strive to know my shames and praises from your tongues. No one else has ever explained that to me, I intone sarcastically, but you don't hear tone. It's actually riveting, how oblivious you are to my interest level—no, it's not. You think you'd sense my four attempts to change the subject away from "the no rights or wrongs" of dating students. Into the profound abyss of your egoism I throw attempts at dialogue, at mutuality. They careen into the gulf between you and others' voices, where your apathy for my address transforms, in mid-air, my generous responses into criticisms you blank and to flattery you hear. Your ears are stopped with arrogance; your mouth could use a cork. How familiar with the manly neglect of female input am I! Since I got regularized, I now dispense with the expected, pretty deferences. Your attentions are not so strongly in my purpose bred, that all the world besides methinks are dead!

CXXXIX

O! Don't call me bystander! Don't make me struggle to justify my silence before the wrongs that the golf-shirted confederacy do. Your unkind witness lays a doily upon my heart; you wound me. I'm not a white-right thug, not violent. They are brutes; their whiteness has nothing of my enlightened schooling. You confuse their abuse of power with my power, and slay me with ungracious evaluation. I buy Inuit art; don't tell me that's not enough. My love is invested elsewhere; I banish brutes from consciousness; my sight allows all my dear heart can take. For bearing ill will toward ugliness just stokes angers; I protect my shine from anxiety. When a friend's aside shows a little hate, you need to just ignore it, rather than open up wounds with accusation. Why ruin a nice evening, when they might be going through something tough at work, when they're human family otherwise? Oppression is a big word; anyone would get defensive at being called tyrannical. I need to bide my time; I need to let stews simmer; I need to excuse myself from this seat at the table. I want a home rosy with love; I want to be sure my little girl knows her pretty looks aren't shameful. I've been open-minded; I don't want enemies, and yet, here you are, throwing forefathers' old missteps in my face. Maybe it's your hard feeling that turns family into foes. Making everything about what white bogeymen do is ugliness; it's reverse-painting all white people. I am overwhelmed right now; how dare you suggest that the irreparable injuries liberal democracy has met do not scorch my soul! I am able-bodied, too, do you then say I oppress the handicapped? Really, Sonnet, I am nearly suicidal watching the news. If I'm so bad, kill me outright for my white shameful looks, and rid the savage planet of my needless compassion.

CL

O! from what power the rapist wants his sorry to be enough. The rapist's powerful friends, mighty with representation, ink a suffering conscience their way. They want to muzzle my heart, to sway my stand, to make me give their lies grace, gaslight my own true sight, and swear that their brothering hasn't enabled their brother's sadistic offsides. It's his birthday—come on, you won't disgrace the day with old offences, when he wants to throw us all this party? say brothers and their groomed companions. Speaking of offensive things makes us ill, stirs hatreds in the family's covert pysche: we refuse confrontation with buddy's deeds, when there is such strength in our propaganda. Meanwhile, the scared rapist can't exorcise the spectre of his act. He'd kill the account—that's all in my mind—by threatening my mind's worth. His unaccountability depends on fellow bullies' tacit sexcapade endorsement and bitches like me who've been taught to heel. He wonders how to make me love him—love, the most effective mollifier. Love, that tenders the most reconciliatory heart. Can't my hard eyes see his remorse? Are bygones just cause of hate? Meanwhile, I've got to hold a job while I ugh his love delusion, while his associated brothers doorkeep. If I work with his brothers (and who aren't his brothers?), am I disgusting? Should I disgust myself, for not abhorring their money and state? I feel my filthy unworthiness every day, that I pay my bills without decolonizing everything that touches me. #MeToo, write workers-through-the-mindfuck of property. We will be untroubled only where we know ourselves, beloved, of the earth.

Check Your Privilege!

MARIE CARRIÈRE

There is a *thing* that some are still somehow able to refer to as CanLit without cringing. Two-Spirited Trans poet Gwen Benaway even broke up with that *thing* for being too exclusive, too white, too old, too exploitative, too heteronormative, and too humourless—in a wonderfully smart, funny, badass essay that appeared in *carte blanche* in 2017.[1] For the sake of metaphor, let's just call this *thing* a *field*, and what have been called the Galloway-Boyden-Atwood-Niedzviecki "dumpster fires" recently ablaze in it have had me thinking about intersectionality.[2] Focused on the interconnection (rather than simple juxtaposition or hierarchy) of race, gender, and class, and also of sexuality, age, ability, and other categories of marginalization, intersectionality is a mode of feminist analysis of the various kinds of social oppression that are so often the bedrock of injustice and violence.

In particular, what's been stuck in my craw is the white neo-liberal pushback against intersectional resistance to the entitlement and privilege lurking in the underbrush, through tropes like "call-out culture," "check-your-privilege" memes, and a recent horror show: the alt-right's defence of "free speech" in light of the Lindsay Shepherd debacle at Wilfrid Laurier University, and the administrative and all-around stupidity that entailed from that mess.[3] But let me begin with a personal anecdote that reflects, I think, both the idea of intersectional work and the retaliation it almost instantly seems to draw—often in the name of freedom of speech, as well as badly, or hardly, veiled white (most often) male privilege.

This past spring, I was invited to deliver a public lecture on the feminist ethics of care, in Vancouver, to a Francophone women's cultural group called Réseau-Femmes. I was delighted, and nervous, about the challenge of making my academic research and writing accessible to a wider audience, let alone one concerned with the everyday labour and care practices of women. I decided to test parts of my presentation on a few readers from my personal circle, *id est* my mom in the first instance, and a close friend as my second reader. My talk began with this:

Je suis une nord-américaine blanche, allochtone, bourgeoise, instruite, littéraire, et féministe. Je suis une femme cisgenre, c'est-à-dire, l'identité de mon genre correspond à mon sexe. Mon privilège social est ostensible et indéniable. Je suis fille d'une mère et d'un père; je suis moi-même mère de deux filles; je suis conjointe, amie, et confidente. J'ai un chien, un chat, parfois un poisson, et trois mois sur douze, une roseraie et un potager. Je suis mentore, administratrice, parfois poète; je suis essayiste et professeure. Le soin est au cœur de ma vie.

[I am a white, settler, bourgeoise, educated, literary, feminist, North American woman. I am a cis woman, that is to say, my gender identity corresponds to my sex. My social privilege is apparent and undeniable. I am the daughter of a mother and a father; I myself am the mother of two daughters; I am a partner, friend, and confidante. I have a dog, a cat, sometimes a fish, and three months of the year, a rose and vegetable garden. I am a mentor, an administrator, sometimes a poet; I am an essayist and a professor. Care is at the heart of my life.][4]

My introduction was meant to be both political and lighthearted. Situating myself and my privilege as a white, North American, settler, middle-class, educated, cis woman constituted, of course, the political, indeed inter-sectional, gesture; the references to domestic pets and tasks that occupy, as do my daughters and students, my own daily caregiving practices elic-ited kind, knowing laughter from my audience. As for my mom, she loved it: "*J'aime beaucoup beaucoup.* [i.e., She really liked it!] *Je trouve que c'est une belle approche à ton sujet.*" After all, she's my mom, you might say. But when she's in disagreement, she doesn't mince words.

And so I decided to go ahead with the opening remarks—despite my second reader, who had emailed me the following a few days before:

> I will admit that I find your introductory comments about your own privilege to be overly apologetic. I know that acknowledging privi-lege seems to be the thing to do these days, but I don't agree with the trend. Let's say that I am a critically minded member of a racial minority group and that I am reading your essay. How am I in any way helped or reassured by a confession of white privilege? To me it sounds rote and contrived, sort of the way we have to sing the national anthem before a hockey game. I simply don't buy that the confession of white privilege actually makes a difference or opens up room for a more genuine conversation between equals.

Ayoye. My friend didn't mince words either. I was staggered by that reaction, but wasn't exactly surprised or really dismayed, or at least not enough to exclude acknowledging my social privilege from my text. As another good friend reminded me, my reader's searing point of view indirectly recalls Vivek Shraya's own questioning of the practice of acknowledging Indige-nous territory in her poem "indian," from the collection *even this page is white*. "is acknowledgment enough?" asks the poet-speaker; "i *acknowledge i stole this*/but i am keeping it social justice/or social performance."[5]

Am I being one of those "good white people" who Afro-American writer Brit Bennett in turn does not exactly chastise but does problematize in a 2014 essay?[6] Am I one of those who tend to co-opt and detract from Black or Indigenous narratives with their good, but ineffectual, if not self-congratulatory, intentions?

Recently, I've noticed some disturbing backlash to the privilege issue bouncing around social media. One form appears in a meme that is a riff off Donald Sutherland's role in the 1978 remake of *Invasion of the Body Snatchers*. Decontextualized as most internet memes tend to be, we are faced with an old angry white guy yelling the words, "CHECK YOUR PRIVILEGE" and pointing accusingly into the camera. I suppose it's supposed to be funny, and ironic, and thoroughly dismissive. Personally, I find it a grotesque, revolting image, with the ugly resonance of the right's co-opting of political correctness, and again, as we've seen recently at Wilfrid Laurier University, free speech, in order to silence minority voices demanding to be heard, respected, and recognized. Those voices have been particularly resonant, with the #MeToo campaign, which Tarana Burke founded more than ten years ago, and which regenerated this past year in unprecedented ways in turn in the wake of the pervasiveness of sexual harassment and sexual violence finally surfacing from the substratum not only of Hollywood, mass media corporations, and professional sport, but of the everyday workplace where women of colour as well as trans, Indigenous, white and Black women and girls work, lead, mentor, and study.

Getting back to my second reader, what shook me wasn't so much the questioning of what was considered a trivial trend. Like acknowledging territory, stating my privilege as a white feminist academic surely is not enough to decolonize our heteronormative, white-supremacist patriarchies. It was my friend's assumption that my address was meant to help or reassure racialized people in the room. I'm not sure what it says about me that it never occurred to me that this was my goal in acknowledging my privilege. Particularly in the context of francophone scholarship, in which I actively participate, the practice isn't common at all, just as acknowledging territory—a long precolonial tradition among First Peoples—from a settler point of view isn't common either, at least not in Quebec.

But whether in an English- or French-speaking setting, I'm convinced, at least at this point in time, that drawing attention to my racial, class, and gender privilege as well as my settler occupancy of treaty or unceded ancestral lands has the effect of destabilizing, maybe even of annoying, and hopefully of prompting critical reflection. Intersectionality is, after all, at the heart of any *situated, material, and embodied* idea of care, which was the topic of my talk. The intertwined workings of race, class, and gender are central to an understanding of care as a practice and an ethics for our time, and even, as care philosopher Joan Tronto argues, to a possible though never guaranteed solution to the problem of difference that has divided feminist theory sometimes beyond repair: "the perspective of an ethic of care is crucial in feminist theory; caring requires that one start from the standpoint of the one needing care or attention. It requires that we meet the other morally, adopt that person's—or group's—perspective and look at the world in those terms. In this regard, caring becomes a way to monitor, and perhaps to check, the bad faith that might otherwise creep into the activities of feminist theorists."[7] Despite the past thirty years of intersectional feminism, keeping interweaved categories of oppression in view is still no mean feat. Recent revisiting of intersectional analysis by such pioneering critics of this methodology, including Kimberlé Crenshaw, have drawn attention to that very fact.[8]

I guess, in the end, I was trying to put my proverbial money where my mouth was.

This all may sound like a sweaty exercise in self-justification. Maybe it is, but I am actually okay with that. My friend's reaction—and I am thankful for it—prompted me to think harder about not only the practice of acknowledging social privilege and colonial space but on its possibly unwanted effects on the persons who receive that acknowledgement.

How might the Indigenous individuals in my audience have received this white settler woman's acknowledgement of the unceded territory of the Musqueam people in Vancouver, or of the Coast Salish Nation in Victoria, where I also lectured during the same trip? Are those speech acts for them?

They already know too well that settlers are occupying their unceded lands. Who's it for, then? Maybe other settlers in the room who need unsettling— just as I do, regularly, repeatedly, in my daily goings-on, in my daily acts of care and occasional descents into not caring enough—just as my mostly white settler students do in my Canadian Literature classroom. Here, incidentally, I currently acknowledge territory at the start of every class. *i acknowledge i stole this.* Hopefully I am teaching my students, as they themselves volunteer to acknowledge territory once we are deeper into our semester, that saying so is not nearly enough.

And so, I write this personal essay as a white settler cis woman, privileged in my middle-class upbringing and living. I am not apologizing. I situate myself and my privilege at this particular time in our history, which is, maybe in more deflected ways but also more than ever, precarious and whitewashed and male-dominated and colonial AF. I don't think I am congratulating myself for making this awareness public. I am an ally—yes, I still believe in the potential of this term—to, and not a representative of, minority and Indigenous voices.

I am drawing your attention to the ways in which I walk through the world, trying to figure out how to resist the indignities that befall my sex and gender, trans people, First Peoples, queer and minority groups, and children, all over the world and right under our stupid noses.

I'll continue to share drafts with my trusted second reader, and with my mom (because she loves me). I will most likely continue to be challenged. We'll talk, disagree, and hear, respect, and recognize one another.

We all need so much more of that.

refuse: a trans girl writer's story

KAI CHENG THOM

they asked me to write something
for this anthology about "refusing CanLit"
to be honest
i did it for the $75
that toronto rent ain't cheap
and job security for trans girls
is shaky in the best of times
(and i am
one of the lucky ones)

can you refuse something
that was never offered to you?
can you reform/remake/revolutionize
a place you never lived in?
let me tell you
about the place where i lived
and my writing grew
like dandelions in a trash heap

i grew up in east van
not the trendy part
where hip white queer writers live
but the immigrant part
full of asians
where english is not the default
and the word "CanLit"
is part of no one's vocabulary

i wasn't a word
in "CanLit's" vocabulary either
not me, a skinny chinese fag
growing up weedy
bespectacled, dressed in
bargain bin sweatpants and
a hand me down disneyland hoodie
looking surreptitiously
for gay reading material
in a public library branch

i mean, seriously
crack open "CanLit"
how many skinny chinese fags
can you find?
maybe one, an underdeveloped
subplot in a Wayson Choy novel?
and how many sad white women
languishing exquisitely
in rural towns
sublimating repressed sexuality
into an emotional resonance
with woodland creatures?
i rest my case

they tell me that the university
creative writing departments in canada
are rife with male professors who abuse
their power
to sexually harass and assault
innocent young women
i do not doubt that this is true
it is the nature of power and men
to misuse and abuse bodies
so i'll take your word for it
though i must admit that i
have never been
to a university creative writing department
i have never been that kind
of innocent young woman
places like that
were never made
for bodies like mine

sometimes white writer friends
tell me they are shocked
by all the scandals
currently going on in canadian
literary circles
i always want to say
i am shocked that you are shocked
what kind of world
did you think we were living in?
but then i remember
that they are white people
which means they might have grown up

believing
that they are entitled to safety
to this thing you call justice

god, i must sound really cynical
what with all this ranting
you probably can guess
where i'm going with this:

it's hard for me to care
about reforming "CanLit"
about making it a "safer space"
for "diverse and marginalized voices"
because for fuck's sake the whole thing
is a settler colonial project
that is designed to gobble up
anything that it deems
powerful or precious

it's hard to care about
some abstract national
culture-building project
when last month in toronto
they found the body
of a dead trans girl in a ravine
reported but left to rot
by social service providers
and the police
like something no one wanted
someone no one cared about

what happens to the ones
who have never been seen
as powerful or precious?
the ones that canada doesn't want
that "CanLit" doesn't care about

we are ones who are refused
we are the refuse
the garbage
(did you know
that an internet slang word
for trans girl is "trash girl"?)
like all the other bodies
(Indigenous
racialized
transsexual
disabled)
that this country
used up, stepped on
threw away

so no i am not interested in "CanLit"
"CanLit" is a nation building project
the bones of my ancestors
that still lie buried beneath
the Canadian Pacific Railway say
that my people have a bad history
with nation building projects
and if there's anything my family
has taught me
it is to know
when you are getting the short end
of a shitty deal

you may think that i am cynical
i am not cynical
i am a believer in refuse
in garbage, in trash
i want to celebrate
that which has been thrown away—

tattered flowers, dismembered limbs
the rotting scraps
of things that a nation leaves behind
i want to imagine a time and place into being
that is more than "CanLit"
ever could be
something wilder, freer
than what is allowed to exist
in creative writing departments
and polite literary conferences

i want to know what grows
in the places where
we buried the bones

When a Cow Saves Your Life, You Learn that Audre Lorde Is Always Right

DOROTHY ELLEN PALMER

On March 1, 2018, I had open-heart surgery to replace my aortic valve. Today, I owe my life to a cow and to the skill of cardiac surgeons who transplanted a healthy bovine valve into my failing human heart. As I fight my way back from that kind of fear and fog, priorities become clear. I hug my children with new joy and gratitude, but also realize that sentimentalizing near-death experience reduces the potential for transformative reflection. For me, after having my heart stopped, repaired, and restarted, the vital takeaway is this: we demean our hearts when we reduce them to love and kindness. The heart is a courage pump. It generates the beating hope with which we take heart. It empowers our heart's desire. Now that medical science has given me another few years to find mine, I vow to use the time left me courageously.

I'm going to stop pretending I have forever to make change. I don't.

I'm sixty-three. Born in 1955. I've never gone anywhere gently. I'm a disabled senior, a retired English/drama teacher, union activist, and an adoptee who spent her whole life searching for her birth parents. I long to integrate these identities. Unfortunately, the scar slicing my chest embodies the painful split between CanLit and my disabled community. As I heal, I dream of a reknitted body: a committed cadre of folks disabled and abled, working together for change. But now that it appears I'm too stubborn to die, please don't "heart" me. What I really want is an answer to this question: as I fight to return to CanLit, will there be a place for me in it?

There is no point claiming we want a new CanLit unless we together find the courage to envisage two things: how to dismantle its current formation and what we want to build in its place. Post-surgery, as I tried to imagine a diversity that equally includes all marginalized voices, I did as I have done since I first encountered her work in 1979: I turned to Audre Lorde.

In my twenties, I'd never read a Black, womanist, activist poet, never conceived of a disabled writer who embraced her disabilities. After her mastectomy, Lorde refused a prosthesis, writing: "Either I love my body one breasted now or remain forever alien to myself." With advanced myopia, Lorde was legally blind, but her vision of women as warriors, her examination of her intersecting oppressions as a Black, working-class, aging, disabled lesbian, her work to fuse social justice with righteous anger, all made her a personal role model for forty years. Now that I'm a single, impoverished, fat old woman on a walker, I'm standing proof of her visionary clarity that we don't live single-oppression lives. I'd often pondered this piece of advice, but it took heart surgery for me to finally get it: "You can't dismantle the master's house using the master's tools."

This is the error I made fighting CanLit's dumpster fires: I used the wrong tools.

To fight UBCAccountable, the appropriations of Joseph Boyden, and the vile suggestion that there should be an Appropriation Prize, I should have retooled my activism. By nature and by nurture, I'm a fighter. I'm a feisty little bastard born to a mentally ill, working-class, single mother. My adoptive parents refused to pay for university for a girl, especially for one who wasn't really theirs. Thanks to scholarships, I became a teacher in 1982. Over three decades, as a career-long unionist, as an Ontario Secondary School Teachers' Federation branch president, I joined and initiated fights against homophobia, racism, sexism, sexual harassment, and bullying. As picket captain, I led walkouts and strikes. I got punched and spat on when I stuck my head into cars asking drivers not to cross our line. As a disabled writer, I've had CanLit colleagues pat me on the head and claim they can write about marginalized groups to which they do not belong because they will use "empathy" and "good research." I've called all my colleagues out about the harm and hypocrisy of attending inaccessible literary events. These are the tools I needed to fight fires with firepower.

On November 14, 2016, when a letter appeared that author Joseph Boyden, in defence of his good friend Steven Galloway, called "An Open Letter to UBC: Steven Galloway's Right to Due Process," with eighty-some CanLit "glitterati" signatures attached, it made me want to start singing Mr. Cockburn's little ditty about a rocket launcher. Instead, I made the critical error of fighting without one. On my blog and on Facebook, good-teacher-me micro-explained how I believed the UBCAccountable letter substituted celebrity for expertise.[1] I asked UBCAccountable to do their homework, to research the democratic due processes already enjoyed by Galloway: a negotiated employment contract, free union representation, the right to grieve dismissal, a provincial arbitration process, and the protections of labour and privacy law. Instead, UBCAccountable called for their own version of "due process," which holds, dangerously, that private employee information can be made public. When UBCAccountable supporters leaked an unverifiable version of a report about Galloway by the University of British Columbia's consultant—retired Supreme Court Judge Mary Ellen Boyd—I did my best to counter what some UBCAccountable signatories said about information they alleged was in the document. Whenever UBCAccountable supporters claimed, with Galloway's lawyer, that Galloway's relationship with the Main Complainant was nothing but "an affair,"[2] I referred them to the press release of the the Main Complainant's lawyer alleging sexual harassment and abuse.[3] I kept asking other questions about the reasons for the UBCAccountable website and open letter, and what the long-term goals of Galloway's legal team actually were. Believing as teachers do, that if listeners don't get it, it's my fault. I kept explaining. I wrote some twenty-thousand words.

My explications joined many other heartfelt attempts to reach UBCAccountable signatories as we attempted to share our beliefs that what they were doing was wrong. Feminists did exemplary research, detailing the connections between theory and practice. Hundreds of statements flooded social media, requesting accountability and empathy from UBCAccountable signatories. More than six hundred people signed a counter-letter supporting complainants, survivors, and sexual assault workers, asking signatories to unsign the UBCAccountable open letter.[4] Some did unsign it. But too many chose to ignore the anguish they had triggered. When challenged, many doubled down. Those of us who asked hard questions about what might be the real function of the UBCAccountable open letter had our careers and persons threatened, but the only harm many UBCAccountable supporters saw was one they claimed but never documented: they said that signatories were called "rape apologists" on social media.[5] In this, they displayed touching empathy, for Mr. Galloway and each other.

With the arrival of the 2018 #MeToo movement to support survivors and identify sexual harassment perpetrators, I suspect some UBCAccountable supporters realized they'd picked the wrong side of history. Despite that choice, many of them thrived. They got agents and book contracts. They headlined literary festivals. They won prestigious prizes. One strutted like a diva on a Hollywood red carpet. When some even got teaching jobs despite being on public record as disbelieving students who report sexual harassment, that's when it hit me. If publishers are like school boards, signatories of UBCAccountable are like principals. They aren't in the union and don't want to be. They snuggle up to power to benefit from its glow. They espouse the myth of merit and prioritize personal ambition. UBCAccountable aimed and fired the double barrels of colonialism and capitalism with which middle-class, white, abled CanLit has historically armed its members. They endorsed and reinforced a system of scarcity that fosters competition and celebrity, that enshrines the misogyny, white privilege, ableist privilege, and whisper networks by which a who-knows-who hierarchy confers rewards and reproduces itself.

And, while they comfortably carried all the weaponry of that hierarchy, I may have reached other readers, but as for reaching UBCAccountable, I effectively wasted two years shooting blanks. Persuasion proved a useless tool because it can never penetrate privilege. No one ever gives up status and financial advantage simply because underlings ask politely, using empathy and good research. No hierarchy cedes power until they are forced to do so.

It took a personal second example of CanLit weaponry in action before I found my own tools. In 2017, when reporter Jorge Barrera at APTN outed Joseph Boyden, the author of the UBCAccountable open letter, on multiple charges of plagiarism[6]—as discussion of his plagiarized identity evolved—I amplified Indigenous commentators on social media who discussed the revelations, but knew it would have been inappropriate to insert myself. I'm a white woman. I have no seat at any Indigenous table. Indigenous communities have the sole right to evaluate, claim, or not claim Boyden as they see fit. In post-surgery retrospect, however, to my regret, I also held back from speaking up on another topic: how settler Canada shrugged at an imposter, one who cavalierly adopted an identity not his own and hurt adoptees in the process.

The Adoption Council of Canada cites seven million, or one in five Canadians, as touched by adoption.[7] Having joined several adoption-rights organizations over four decades, having helped many adoptees, all torn from kin and culture, I know we embody adoption trauma all our lives. We have higher rates of depression, addiction, divorce, and suicide, with Indigenous adoptees paying the highest costs of all. The Canadian Church and State have stolen children from young, poor, unwed, unwell, disabled, Indigenous, and racialized mothers for centuries. They have long colluded in bastard erasure and premeditated Indigenous genocide. In "the sixties scoop," they illegally seized twenty thousand Indigenous children. Today, Black and Indigenous children are still seized disproportionately, and are still placed predominantly in white homes.[8]

I am in no way challenging what adoption or other forms of welcoming mean to Indigenous communities. What I do challenge is what Boyden appeared to hope his self-arranged adoption might mean to settler Canada.

For much of his working life, during which he accepted well-compensated spokesperson roles, Joseph Boyden claimed Indigenous ancestry. But APTN reporters did their research well: his claim could not be substantiated by Indigenous history or settler genealogy. He had no aunties at that time; no Indigenous nation or community claimed him. When he was exposed, he didn't pursue "adult welcoming" as a way to be claimed by an Indigenous community. In what many Indigenous commentators criticized as an attempt to make a shortcut end run around accountability, he was "adopted" by the family of an Ojibwa filmmaker and friend.[9] To this settler adoptee, he also appeared to be using the settler language of adoption in the hopes that settlers would now see him as Indigenous. Such an act is in no way comparable to the racist cultural appropriation of Indigeneity, but on the day the announcement was made, I saw it as an attempt to appropriate a second marginalized identity to shore up his first appropriated identity.

I know what my adoption means to me. Before age three, I had had seven foster homes and two long stays in convalescent hospitals. As a ward of the state, I was the victim of infant sexual abuse. I can never name my abusers, but my body won't let me forget or forgive them. I'm a permanently angry product of trauma. I lived half a century with my adoption file sealed. At fifty-three, I learned my mother's name. I met her once before she died. I'd given up all hope of finding my father. Thanks to DNA testing, I found him literally twenty-four hours before my heart surgery, six months after he died. My adopted lifetime is defined by pain and loss.

Joseph Boyden is a middle-aged man who grew up in the Toronto suburb of Willowdale with two birth parents, full and half-siblings, and full-blood relatives.[10] When anyone appropriates an identity not their own, they do so on the backs of those with lifelong, authentic struggle.

How does it make adoptees feel to have someone cavalierly appropriate our pain?

For "sympathy." For attention. For publicity. For profit and personal gain.

And settler Canada bought it. Shrugging at his appropriations and his claims, settler Canada either believed him or preferred him to keep on being what Indigenous critics call a "pretendian."[11] Given that white, abled CanLit appears to prefer palatable imposters to finding new and accessible space for disabled writers, I'm wondering if some abled writers might attempt a copycat fraud themselves. With "empathy" and "good research," with disabled mentors, with a cane or crutch as a prop, an abled writer could easily impersonate a disabled one. Especially if you were a charming, good-looking, well-educated, white man. A good little Tiny Tim, one who never utters the words *ableism* or *ableist fragility*. If you don't challenge the complicity of readers and writers who organize, read at, and attend inaccessible literary events, then abled CanLit would embrace you precisely because you embodied their entitlement to the historic unfair advantages of ableist privilege.

This is what mere words can't fight: the racist weaponry of the Appropriation Prize.

The premise within it is vile: that authenticity is "a joke." That white, abled entitlement trumps diversity. That all writing jobs must be open to abled, white folks at all times. That impersonators are preferred precisely because they make abled, white employers and client readers comfortable.

One reason the CanLit industry behaves this way is because it has never faced financial consequences for its lack of diversity. Writers don't identify as workers, but as self-employed professionals. The big employers of CanLit get generations of obedient, ambitious worker bees eager to write for less than minimum wage. Big employers don't much care if lowly worker-writers are exploited. They will nod at accessibility, diversity, and social justice, throw us an occasional, politically correct bone, and go back to stoking a competitive star system that prioritizes profits. Most sadly, some writers participate in their own oppression. When they shrug at inaccessibility and inauthenticity, when they compete in the Oppression Olympics, or step back from solidarity, they're identifying with the employer. They are reinforcing the racist, ableist hierarchy, as if it will enrich and protect them.

But Audre Lorde is always right: Silence is always complicit. It protects no one.

Unless writers organize, unless and until we make loud, collective demands with clear financial consequences that hit the employers of CanLit in their wallets, nothing will change.

Do you want to see the employers of CanLit continue to defer diversity, to offer its colonizing "kindness," by siphoning off and absorbing a few, token, anointed, marginalized writers, or do you want the hierarchical formation that is CanLit dismantled and rebuilt anew?

The effectiveness of Roxane Gay removing her book from a publisher about to publish a fascist tells us that the principled withdrawal of our labour works. If writer-workers unite to use the tools of identity activism and collective bargaining to demand fair hiring, we could negotiate from collective strength. We could tell Publisher Employers that if they do not meet our diversity quotas for all marginalized groups, if they instead try to publish imposters, we will take collective action. We will not appear with authors who appropriate identities not their own. We will not buy their books. We will flood social media asking the public not to buy them. We'll picket every launch, reading, and festival. Then we won't work for non-progressive publishers at all. We will withhold our new books until they meet our demands. Until the industry of CanLit negotiates a fair collective agreement for all, we'll stay on strike.

Is the dream of a militant writers' union my post-surgery pie-in-the-sky?

Currently, yes. But in their day, so were "anti-slavery," "votes for women" "universal health care," the forty-hour workweek," "a woman's right to choose," and "equal marriage." Writers have the right to demand the twenty-first-century working conditions won by other workers. The lessons of activist history and the wisdom of Audre Lorde are clear: We must forge new tools. We must share the courage to demand collective, collaborative justice, now, in our lifetimes. We must take heart.

CanLit Hierarchy vs. the Rhizome
A DISCUSSION BETWEEN NATALEE CAPLE AND NIKKI REIMER

Why the rhizome? I wanted, in essay format, to talk about some of the problems endemic to the structures of hierarchy, celebrity, and scarcity that I've witnessed over my nearly twenty years writing in Canada, but I was struggling with the structure and felt like I was writing in circles. As per usual when I hit a block of some kind, I posted on Facebook something to the effect of "OMG help I don't know what I'm doing haha." Pal Natalee Caple offered to look at what I'd pulled together and suggested that a dialogue might provide a useful scaffolding on which to structure my thoughts. We proceeded to chat back and forth over email. I wanted to start with the rhizome because the model of Vancouver's Rhizome Café was something I saw as having successfully created an alternative and independent community where respect and social justice could be foregrounded. I thought that maybe it would be useful to think of a writing community as a rhizomatic structure, instead of as a system of popularity, awards, and sales winners and losers. What follows is an edited version of our rhizomatic discussion.

NC: Can you describe what a "rhizomatic community" looks like and what you think the benefits are?

NR: Though I'm aware of the Deleuze and Guattari concept, I'm thinking here of the model of Rhizome Café, one of my favourite hangout spots in

Vancouver circa 2008–12. I'm using the definition from the café's website: a "horizontal root system... [t]he plant sends shoots up from nodes in the rhizome, creating what look like many separate plants. These seemingly unrelated individuals are actually all connected, through a system that's not immediately visible to the eye."[1] Co-owners and partners Lisa Moore and Vinetta Lenavat curated a space where every event that took place aligned with their own values, with community and social justice at the forefront. Vancouver writer Meredith Quartermain created a monthly dinner for local women and visiting writers there—we called ourselves "the Rhizomatics"—that was to me very nurturing.

These dinners were not big actions, and, from an intersectional lens, they weren't as inclusive as they could have been, which is a shortcoming, but in an industry where a lot of the power is still in the hands of cis men—though a lot of grunt work in literary production is performed by women—the Rhizomatics dinners provided a sense of community and safety. I feel like there's a lot of potential in forming a literary community after the model of these dinners, and of the café itself, and while there are so many amazing organizations in Canada doing this type of work—the FOLD festival,[2] *Room* magazine[3]—Canadian Literature as we've been talking about it publicly over the last several years is extremely neo-liberal and hierarchical; think of the major transnational publishers for whom CanLit is a marketing hook. I'm exploring "CanLit" here in terms of literary production, marketing and media coverage, and I'm considering the mainstream and popular to be what sits at the top of the hierarchy, and what is most visible to the non-writing public. (Recognizing that there is no one accepted definition of CanLit...). The fallout from the last couple of years—specifically the feuding that has occurred over mass media, social media, and blogs—has made it clear that some people will go to great lengths to defend their positions as bestselling writers, powerful publishers, and well-known tastemakers within this structure.

NC: How would you position yourself in Canadian Literature? Where do you think you belong in the hierarchy you describe?

NR: I'm never quite sure how to reckon with my own positioning within CanLit—do I have status? How much? How little? I've been more or less active in literary communities in Canada for about eighteen years. I've published two books, never won a prize, have never gone into second printing, can't get verified on Twitter. Small potatoes, as far as cultural currency goes. I look at younger writers with as many or more works in print, with rising status, and think I'm not producing fast enough, or not producing quality work. Though there have been periods of time where I've been very active in community/volunteer work—running reading series, producing zines, organizing, hosting—I've entirely internalized the neo-liberal turn toward market capitalism as the only worthy valuation. Shameful to admit, but there it is. Lately I've been privately referring to myself as a "D-List" writer, amusing myself with the thought that my place in the pantheon is equivalent to has-been celebrities like Janice Dickinson[4] or Carrot Top.[5]

NC: Why is it shameful? Is that something a different kind of community could change?

NR: The shame comes from having an ideological opposition to CanLit's culture of celebrity, while still desperately wanting to feel like I belong. I tell myself that I could have done more with all this time, produced a greater volume of better-calibre work if I'd had better and earlier mental health intervention and support, but on the other hand, far sicker, and more marginalized, people have been far more productive than I.

Over the past year or so, as the workings of power within CanLit have revealed themselves in starker relief than we've previously seen, it has occurred to me that what we refer to as "CanLit" is a multi-tiered system of power, influence, reputation, selling power, and fame. I see it as a pyramid of fame and compensation: most of the activity is produced by the most people, on the bottom of the pyramid, but these folks are mostly unknown outside of and even within the field, and they make little to no money for their efforts. Mid-tier activity is a smaller group of people, making some money, with books put out by small/indie presses. At the very top are the "superstars," of whom we're only allowed to have a few (because a small population like Canada can only support so many; because mid-level presses have been bought out by big conglomerates; because Canadian tall poppy syndrome,[6] etc. etc.). They make living wages off their writing, as opposed to those who labour in other fields and try to get the writing done in between, and their names have cachet outside of the writing community. Your mom has heard of them: Atwood. Boyden. Ondaatje. (There are, of course, multiple gradations between the three tiers I mention.)

NC: I think there is a lot of smoke and mirrors in publishing about money and who is a "superstar." Most writers in Canada have other jobs, and even the most famous, who may have cachet with media and, yes, with readers and scholars, signal a lot of their importance by association. And fame in CanLit does not stretch far outside of our world. This is where I see the danger of prize culture and celebrity—it is so precarious and so underscored by anxiety over its precarity that it requires constant renewal. We have to keep saying the same few names and produce scholarship that supports the argument that we have a canon to maintain an outdated vision of a national literature that is stable and recognizable. A healthy national literature is always changing and renewing, and values—aesthetic, political, social—are re-examined and updated. The great desire for a Canadian canon is a colonial impulse that pushes too many voices out and works harder to maintain hierarchies than it does to examine damaging systemic issues. What we think of as famous established successful Canadian literature does not really represent the breadth of what is happening in Canadian literature, and it minimizes that breadth—the queer literature, the genre work, Indigenous writing, intersectional analysis, feminist and political writing, the mass of works in every genre by people of colour...

NR: Yes, absolutely.

NC: I know you and I both think a lot about free labour and uncredited labour in CanLit. Can you say a bit more about that? I feel like that is one of the locations for abuse of lesser-known writers and beginning writers.

NR: There's this enormous structure of labour underpinning the entire enterprise, but everybody pretends it's an equal and open meritocracy. The locations for abuse are built right into the structure.

So much of literary production and culture in this country exists only because of free and devalued labour, which means that the people doing the work are either wealthy enough that they can afford to put in the free time, or that they take a vow of poverty in order to "do" what they "love." Literary magazines, for example, are largely run on one or two paid positions, a handful of people earning small honoraria, and a small army of unpaid interns and volunteers. (And when you work out the hourly wages of the paid positions and honoraria, it's at or below minimum wage.) But these spaces hold immense cultural capital and prestige, so there is competition to be part of them. Getting to enter the system therefore can occur because of luck and timing or who you know or who you drink with or who you sleep with. It's not always so crass. But it can be, and it can be easily be abused.

And, of course, the labour put forth in these spaces is not only mental and sometimes physical (schlepping boxes, hauling chairs, prepping mailouts), but emotional as well. Trying to thoughtfully curate a reading series or an issue of a literary magazine takes emotional effort that is not visible in the final event or product. Having to thoughtfully deal with abusers who've been revealed to be in your community's midst takes enormous emotional effort and toll. I and many of my friends and peers have really struggled to continue to write in the social environment that has developed.

Most literary festivals make me extremely uncomfortable, because they always seem (to me) to reveal the inner workings of this highly stratified power structure. Volunteers are sold access to cultural capital; in reward, their unpaid labour allows the festival to function. No literary festival in Canada today could operate if it had to pay all of the workers needed for all of the ticket taking and ushering, on-site sales, ferrying of "talent" back and forth from the airport.

Though I'd volunteered for Wordfest when I lived in Calgary, my first "writing" work for a literary festival was as a volunteer blogger for the Vancouver Writers Festival in 2007 and 2008. At the inaugural meeting to discuss the creation of a set of blogger volunteer positions for the festival, someone asked, "Why not get writers to blog?" Director Hal Wake responded that writers would want to be paid.

We festival bloggers were writing—some of us were "wannabe" or "emerging" writers, but we were not "writers." We were paid in access and perks, rather than money. We produced copy that provided on-the-ground reportage of the festival, sexed it up a bit perhaps, but we weren't "real" writers. So much is promised, coerced, and stolen on the premise of access into the "real" writers club. It's not always or not only a matter of paying one's dues, helping others, working hard on the craft of the writing, and eventually seeing your hard work pay off. There are cliques and coteries that provide access to publishing's inner circle, and there are costs involved in gaining access to these coteries, and remaining within their graces.

NC: Writers-not-writers is very much the condition I see promoted by celebrity culture. Those distinctions allow us to fete some writers and protect them from criticism, and to brutally devalue other writers (sometimes treated as hobbyists and/or malcontents if they speak up about the impact of the treatment they receive in mainstream culture). And very often the legitimacy of writers is questioned on purely economic reasoning. Any values that are directly linked to market value/money made must be examined for the systemic flaws that influence those markets. I am speaking here most strongly to racism, heterocentrism, ableism, and of course sexism—voices that protest these issues, especially if their protest puts them in conflict with very established mainstream authors or presses, will face strong pushback and behind-the-scenes punishment. They will be driven away. But those are the voices that are absolutely necessary to really represent who is here writing now and what responsibility writers have as citizens.

NR: Absolutely. We're watching some of this be revealed right now in the American entertainment industry, and we've watched it be revealed throughout the ongoing feuding spurred by the open letter signed by more than eighty prominent writers, publishers, and publicists asking for accountability after UBC's firing of their Creative Writing chair. We watched it come to light after editor Hal Niedzviecki penned an editorial letter titled "Winning the Appropriation Prize" in an Indigenous voices–themed issue of the Writers' Union of Canada's *Write* magazine, whereby he glibly called for writers to write that which they did not know, and perhaps even compete to be the best appropriator, which in turn caused a number of prominent white editors of major Canadian publications to call for the creation of an actual "Appropriate Prize." [Disclosure: I was on the editorial advisory board of *Write* during this issue, and I solicited young writers to consider submitting to the issue. It was not part of the mandate of the volunteer editorial board to review any content of the magazine prior to publication, and I did not see the column until after it was published. I resigned after reading it, because I did and do feel that it was a disrespectful response to the writers whose work appeared in the issue.] I find it telling that writer Stephen Marche tweeted that "everyone in the country who can *actually write well* is on Galloway's side"[7] (emphasis mine), which backs up my earlier point that literary culture in Canada is conceived by many participating in it to be a highly stratified system of winners and losers, writers and not-writers.

And it is the very same system that creates a literary 1% that is both complicit in and complacent on issues of racism, sexism, and assault. If we can only perceive CanLit as a stratified system of celebrity, then we are going to continually put a few people high up on pedestals. And there will then be entire economies at risk if those superstars suffer any loss in economic value, and people willing to fight dirty against that happening.

What would a community look like that still appreciated and valued the work and art created by a human, but did not elevate that human to hero status?

I'd like to be fully transparent and state for the record that most of my efforts within CanLit over nearly two decades were inward-focused and not cognizant of equity, justice, or a world outside my narrow, privileged worldview. I upheld white supremacy. Racist thought is endemic to a white person's upbringing in a white supremacist society; it's incumbent on the individual to work toward dismantling and decolonizing the kyriarchy[8] within their own subconscious. It's only in the last five or so years that I've been more woke to the fact that my woe-is-me D-List status is intersectional with my straight, white, hetero-cis privilege, and I've been actively working (and failing, and trying again) to decolonize my reading practices and my support and promotion of others since.

NC: Oh yeah, me too. And I think I am still working on some serious gaps. Addressing ableism and amplifying the voices of disabled writers is coming to me woefully late.

NR: Me too. I'm now wondering what it might mean to build an ethical, equal, relational community in CanLit, one that is more socialist and communist than capitalist. And if we are rebuilding CanLit, it cannot and should not be privileged, able-bodied settlers like you and I setting all the terms and making all the decisions.

I'm also thinking of Mark Medley's recent *Globe and Mail* piece on prize culture, wherein he argues that Canada has too many literary prizes.[9] Medley quotes Gillian Roberts as saying: "there's a 'colonial mentality that persists' in the Canadian industry, where authors and publishers are constantly wanting to prove themselves against their American and British counterparts."

At Wordfest this past fall, I saw Métis writer Chelsea Vowel in conversation with Joshua Whitehead. In response to a query about the seemingly precarious state of the world in this Trumpian era, she noted that apocalyptic fears are a marker of white privilege. Whereas Indigenous people in North America have "been post-apocalyptic since contact."

I've been thinking about that response a lot. The questions I now want to ask myself, and ask my (white) friends and colleagues, are: How do you mobilize guilt into something productive and useful? What do we build after the garbage fires? How do we refuse the imperative to fit ourselves and our work into a power structure? How do we decentre ourselves?

Here's a point, too, about class and hierarchies within the CanLit world: those who hold tenured professorships, and A-List authors, or both, have a greater amount of security with which to be activist or go public with opinions. Margaret Atwood is not going to lose any book sales for her screeds. Academics who are not or not yet tenure track, and those of us with regular old jill jobs, are imminently fireable and replaceable, especially in the neo-liberal hypercapitalist precarious world of employment that is 2016–17. There are hundreds of smart young communications professionals ready to take my job in a second if I do anything to embarrass my employer, unionized job or not. Every time one of my tweets got embedded in a news story over 2016–17, I panicked for two weeks afterwards about getting fired.

I want to return to the rhizome. I like the idea of destabilizing the structure from underneath, the way a tree root can wreck a sidewalk or a sewer line. I want to be part of dissident groups of writers operating in interconnected pods, holding each other accountable, and collaborating toward a more equitable community.

How Do We Get Out of Here?
An Atwood Scholar, Signing Off

LORRAINE YORK

1. Corners

I take my title, dejectedly, from an old review of John Newlove's poetry that Margaret Atwood published in *Open Letter* back in the spring of 1973, when she was thirty-four years old: "How Do I Get Out of Here?: The Poetry of John Newlove." Atwood was new to literary fame at that time. Having just published *Surfacing* and *Survival* the year before, she was a writer on the rise, a star ascendant. And in this review of a poetic contemporary (he was thirty-five years old), she argued that Newlove's poetry was obsessed with "corners; what they are, what you do in them and how you get out of them." As it turns out, Atwood explained, Newlove's speakers have lots of ideas about how we deal—or don't deal— with corners. For starters, we're not innocent victims of our corners: "That's the worst of it," Atwood explains. "[W]e ourselves are responsible for the negative qualities of the space we find ourselves in... This is the corner, the closed circle, the double bind: we are able to make the world and we have made a bad one" (122). Still, that very perception, Atwood notes, is both "the worst" but "also the beginning of the way out": the "undesirable qualities" of our condition "can perhaps be cancelled out or at least balanced if we can change our point of view, the direction from which we are seeing and therefore creating it" (122). And...how do we do that? "[T]hrough and despite words and from facing the truth" (126).

Leaving aside here for the moment the enormity of the liberal humanist individualism that permeates Atwood's account of Newlove's poetry—and it is an ENORMITY—what has brought this scrap of memory of a scrap of a review to my mind so insistently in recent days has been my reflection on the corner that Margaret Atwood has backed herself into in the weeks and months since November of 2016 when she signed the UBCAccountable letter offering support for Steven Galloway and offering very little for the women who brought harassment complaints against him. But if she's in a corner of her own making, she's by no means sidelined. There, in her corner, she is also operating as a nodal point in the various controversies that are linked to the UBC case in the same way that power is interlinked in literary and other hierarchies. Consider the writer who spearheaded the UBCAccountable letter, Joseph Boyden, whose support for Galloway reignited already-simmering discussions in Indigenous communities about his incommensurate claims of Indigenous ancestry. Consider Atwood's bizarre tweet on November 24, 2016, that consigned to Boyden the power to legitimize the Indigenous identity of others ("Confirmed @josephboyden that Steven Galloway is #indigenous + was adopted. @ubcaccountable Well known but not so far mentioned in the convo"). Or consider the powerful media people, many of whom defended Galloway and Boyden both, who rushed to tweet their support for Hal Niedzviecki's "Appropriation Prize" in the early hours of May 11, 2017.[1] The actors in these overlapping controversies are themselves overlapping intertwined nodes of power in the Canadian literary and media worlds, and in exercising that power to exclude others, they have done considerable harm. They have transgressed the ethical responsibility of the established writer as set out by Walter Benjamin in "Art as a Producer":

> An author who teaches writers nothing teaches no one. What matters, therefore, is the exemplary character of production, which is able, first, to induce other producers to produce and, second, to put an improved apparatus at their disposal. And this apparatus is better,

the more consumers it is able to turn into producers—that is, readers or spectators into collaborators.

By all such measures, Atwood, Boyden, and Galloway, for starters, are failing in their responsibilities as writers, by taking actions that slam the door on early-career writers, saying, in effect, *You cannot belong. You cannot collaborate with us.*

2. Who Cares?

Over a year after the UBCAccountable intervention in the Galloway case, the controversy reached new depths with the publication of Atwood's *Globe and Mail* op-ed of January 13, 2018, "Am I a Bad Feminist?" In that article, Atwood characterized those who criticized her stance on Galloway as vigilante feminists who style themselves right and "good," and all those, like Atwood, who disagree, as "bad." Many early-career writers, especially writers of colour, responded in turn by saying, in effect, who cares? Vowing to tell their stories to those who will listen and be supportive—those who will "induce other producers to produce," many have decided to route themselves around Atwood and the literary hierarchy. In a moving and profoundly thoughtful response to Atwood's op-ed, Jen Sookfong Lee acknowledged her "confusion of feelings" about a writer who deeply influenced her as a young reader and writer. She described Atwood as a woman who has also "talked down to and scolded some of my dearest friends. She had made statements that made it very clear that power, and specifically, her power, was something she was willing to use to silence young women who had very little power at all." Lee's conclusion? Quoting the line from Atwood's *The Journals of Susanna Moodie*, "Resolve: to be both tentative and hard to startle," Lee proclaimed, "The new CanLit is now making its own resolutions. And guess what? We will not be easily startled."

3. Capital

My own. So far I have been writing (as I generally do) as an academic: invested, yes, in a particular perspective on my subject, in this case in the so-called Canlit "dumpster fires" of recent years, but not involved in them. I have been writing as if I am not present but still narrating! And that won't do anymore. I built a successful career, one I've received promotions, and prizes, and honours for, on the basis of work that was partly devoted to the study of Margaret Atwood's writing and her literary celebrity. I need to think about that. From the very beginning, when I first read the UBCAccountable letter, I was certain where I stood: I could not believe that the letter writers had all but erased the women complainants in their rush to empathize with Steven Galloway. By then I was no longer writing about Atwood. I had published *Margaret Atwood and the Labour of Literary Celebrity* five years earlier, in 2013, and felt that was the last thing I had to say about the topic. My interest then was in the way in which literary celebrity in Canada could have highly sophisticated, industrial dimensions to it. The perfect case in point was Atwood. But my work was moving toward celebrity studies beyond the literary sphere and was beginning to explore the relationship between celebrity and affect. While that was happening, I continued to reap the benefits of having made Atwood a distinct part of my academic career: by my count, one book, one edited book of essays, one chapter of another book, four contributions to other people's collections of essays, four journal articles, several reviews of Atwood criticism, seven conference papers. That's a lot. That's investment (the language of banking is intentional)… and I received returns on that investment. Such academic and readerly investments and returns recall Atwood's argument in *Payback: Debt and the Shadow Side of Wealth*, that estimations of debt and repayment are founded on "a human sense of fairness, balance and justice." I made my investment of readerly and academic engagement and labour, gained my returns, but found myself deeply troubled by Atwood's disproportionate empathy with Galloway. This essay is my seeking of an equilibrium of "fairness, balance, and justice."[2]

4. How Do We Get Out of Here?

Who is this "we"? Why does the title of Atwood's review of Newlove haunt me these days, and why do I feel the need to turn her "I" into a "we"?

I have to admit: I want Atwood to get out of her corner. I've given space to the alternate position, that writers who have been silenced by her chillingly discriminatory comments have every reason to write her off, to say, in effect: you no longer matter to us. We will succeed despite you. And yet I find Jen Sookfong Lee's complicated response moving precisely because it places us in the midst of feelings that are anything but clear-cut: the kinds of feelings that can often attend feelings of betrayal by a figure in our intellectual lives who we may have found inspiring. (I here leave space for those who may have never found that inspiration in Atwood, who have found in her works exclusions and unacknowledged privileges, particularly those attending whiteness. And no, I'm not going to close this parenthesis. In light of her power and influence now, I want Atwood to do what she wrote about all those years ago in her review of John Newlove. I want her to stop being so defensive and, instead, consider the possibility that she may be "responsible for the negative qualities of the space [she] find[s herself] in. . . ." I wish she would consider also that this realization may be "also the beginning of the way out." What would that look like? Realizing that she has placed the welfare of Steven Galloway over the welfare of the female complainants when she extended empathy, in the first place, to him and not to them when she signed the UBCAccountable letter. Realizing that her continuing defensiveness, her need to be "right" and for her critics to be "wrong," is widening the painful breach between her, as someone who should be acting as a Benjaminian producer of producers, "an author who teaches writers," and many of the voices who will come to define the future of Canadian literature. She will need to move "through and despite words"—many of them her own—in order to "[face] the truth" and face it humbly. At the time of writing this, the signs are not promising: Atwood and novelist Susan Swan released an online statement March 22, 2018 (wherewearenow2018.ca/), in which they write, "We regret any perception of harm or silencing effects that this decision [to sign the UBCAccountable letter] may have had on other complainants." Atwood and Swan fall in line with the classically problematic apology that proclaims, in effect, that we are sorry that you perceived harm, not that we are sorry that we harmed you. And the rest of this sentence does more harm: "as we regret the misconceptions about and attacks upon the signatories of the Letter." Because, you know, that harm is presented, even grammatically here, as co-extensive with the harm of silencing complainants and survivors.

How do I get out of here? The very question resounds with the signs of my own complicity and my need to make clear my disaffiliation from Atwood's actions of recent years. I'm already "out" of the study of Atwood; I have turned down recent requests for more critical work on her. In turning down requests, I have tried to initiate conversations about UBCAccountable and Atwood's destructive role therein, to little avail. "Here" is that discussion that we need to have. "Here" is where I want to be. And it's where I've taken myself when invited, in recent months, to give keynote papers both here and abroad. The best I can do is to use the measure of academic celebrity I possess to make clear where I stand, and with whom. I need not "get out of *here*" but, on the contrary, to stay in.

"No Appeal"

CHELSEA VOWEL

Reconciliation is a weirdass thing pretty sure CanLit can tell us how to do it feathers to swear in cops to beat land defenders treaty flags on malls to keep us addicted to capitalism

Crown and Indigenous Relations to continue administering poverty and corruption
white guys playing red guys working with white guys doing projects on residential schools celebrated

round dance cynicism tokenistic territorial acknowledgements as de facto cede release surrender here's an oil patch bursary

we believe women we believe you but not you he's our buddy witch hunt twitter mob
hope you weren't planning on making a home here our literature is about you not for you

I love your culture I hate your face here's a drink splashed in it better than a trailor hitch

Canada 150 teach us teach us make us feel guilty it's settler-domming seed
release sweet surrender 50 shades of Grey Owl

tell me all the terrible things so I can be appalled titillated now me and
Beyak have suffered with you maybe now we have PTSD for you

get over it get over it property rights stay off my lawn we don't shake canes
we shoot kids
free speech fist in your gut crowing joy in your twitter feed got what they
deserved I don't see colour

studying you studying your issues can you do it no we must and that's how we
indigenize the academy that's how we write you in you're on the menu agenda

in a year from now we can all relax and pat ourselves on the back for how
much work we did this decolonization gig is sweet hope you liked it.

Part Three:
RE/FUSE

"Emergent discourses . . . produce knowledge that is working at the limit: at the limit in the sense that that kind of knowledge has been repressed in the Canadian national imaginary and, as a result, pushed to the edges of the field; in the sense that the emergence of such knowledge upsets inherited orthodoxies; and in the sense that its emergence does not attempt to replace by default the doxa of received assumptions with new positivism."

—Smaro Kamboureli[1]

What does refusal cost? What gets lost or forgotten when we refuse something wholesale? There are many ways to begin to tackle these questions, and the pieces gathered in this final section do just that. Importantly, the tone here is not one of hope, or of a simple optimism for what comes next after a significant rupture event. Instead, we might characterize these possibilities as *emergent*, in the same way we speak of *emerging* writers. Emergence is in part about newness, certainly, but it is a newness that is pushing back against the limitations, assumptions, and orthodoxies of the established culture. As Smaro Kamboureli observes, emergence is about working at the limits of what can currently be known. Emerging discourses do not establish a new normal, but ask us why we're so attached to normalcy and stability in the first place. Emergence asks what might come from the ruins of CanLit if we don't try to rebuild it back into a stable cultural edifice.

One example of emergence as a counter to restoration is found in Sachiko Murakami's poetry collection *Rebuild*, and its digital companion, *Project Rebuild*. *Rebuild* addresses race, gender, and gentrification in the city; *Project Rebuild* allows any user to "renovate" a poem on the project website. Taken together, the two texts expand how we might think about crafty and insurgent poetics as a means of both intervention into and experience of belonging. If a poem is a rental unit of language, then it carries traces of what the previous tenants thought and felt. In the case of Vancouver, a city with a long history of using public poetry and artistic intervention as protest, the previous tenants haunt both the pages and the city itself. Murakami's lyric moves from re-articulation to renovation, to rebuilding, allowing the writer, reader, and critic to experience "the encounter of what is sensed with what is known . . . in a new but also recognizable way."[2] Refusing stability or the reimposition of order, this collaborative poetic project instead explores the emergent possibilities of rebuilding as resistance.

The third sense of "refuse" adds a slash—re/fuse—to think about putting things back together (fusing) without restoring the original. It suggests a rebuilding that lets the cracks show, that remembers the moment of rupture and doesn't try to plaster over that history. And, as is the case throughout this book, the contributions in this section think these questions through from multiple institutional and personal perspectives: as professors and editors and writers and activists and mentors and students. The multiplicity of these perspectives reminds us not to restore the image of CanLit as a singular community, but to remember its fundamental fragmentation even as we work to envision what might come next.

In her contribution, Laura Moss foregrounds her roles as both professor and editor. Rather than avoiding issues of power in both these roles, Moss addresses them directly as a mode of both refusing the perpetuation of abuses of power and of acknowledging the work that remains. While both teaching and editing can and have been sites of restrictive and abusive power dynamics, Moss calls on a history of feminist and anti-racist work that strives to recognize injustice and consistently work to do better. As the editor of *Canadian Literature*, Moss holds that editorial work can be proactive and that amplifying the scholarship and writing of others is a crucial part of shifting the discourse when it is done with care and with responsible consultation.

Phoebe Wang is also thinking about power and her position within it, but from the perspective of mentorship within the Asian-Canadian writing community. The history of Asian-Canadian literature, like the history of the term "woman of colour," points to a strategic alignment of identities in the interests of solidarity and political force—though it also evokes the way the literary market turns identities into genres so they can attach a BISAC code to people. Nevertheless, Asian-Canadian literature can be linked more to the former than the latter, and to a body of important critical thinking by scholars like Roy Miki, Larissa Lai, Tara Lee, and Lily Cho (as well as to important literature, much of which Wang cites in her piece). Contemporary conversations about Asian-Canadian art and activism are still being driven by communities and collectives, such as the Asian Canadian Writers' Workshop (www.asiancanadianwriters.ca/), the Project 40 Collective (p40collective .ca/), and the Where Are You From? Collective, "an art-based and activism program for people who identify as Asian" (wayfcollective.weebly.com/). Wang shows how mentorship and collective organizing are still building possibilities for emerging writers and emergent literary communities.

To re/fuse is to work for something better while resisting the positivism of hope. A. H. Reaume's work draws on Sophocles's *Antigone*, in which the protagonist's lament is both a political act and a refusal. She is speaking truth to the power that is her uncle, and she is insisting that there are other laws that deserve her allegiance. And she faces consequences for doing so. We might think of Antigone as a version of Sara Ahmed's feminist killjoy, a resistant figure who engages in the necessary and unsettling work of critique, including critique of "happiness, of how happiness is used to justify social norms as social goods."[3] Alongside Ahmed's work, we could add Lauren Berlant's concept of "cruel optimism," which describes how people often become attached to ideas or objects that stand in the way of their thriving. In the context of CanLit, we might look at how some people have become attached to an optimistic view of CanLit as a thriving literary community, rather than noting how CanLit continues to structurally silence, tokenize, exploit, and exclude many voices. In her essay, A. H. Reaume draws on the work of activists like Jael Richardson, Alicia Elliott, and Carrianne Leung, who argue that we must resist the desire to push past critique into optimism. Instead, Reaume joins in the call for allies who are invested in making CanLit more just to engage in the necessary, urgent work of pointing to systemic inequities and demanding that they be changed.

Returning to the setting of the university, literature scholar Jennifer Andrews asks what the relationship is between the study of Canadian literature within the university and the industry called CanLit. Writing from her position within the academy, Andrews works to situate herself in order to demonstrate the ways that "borders" both figurative and literal fundamentally shape the circulation of Canadian literature as a field of study as well as a field of pedagogy and research. Asking how she herself as a teacher and researcher might work to refuse the restrictive aspects of border-keeping, Andrews signals the importance of a more robust understanding of both the academy and the industry. Further, by thinking through other kinds of centralities—namely those that hinge on "prestige" and geography—Andrews gestures toward more ways in which borders of the imagination take on a very palpable and problematic function. How, she asks, might those working in the academy teach the history of cultural and political borders more productively?

The university as an institution is central in a different way to writers and activists Kristen Darch and Fazeela Jiwa's conversation, as they think through the UBCAccountable controversy as an event that can be placed alongside other events—including the Writing Thru Race conference—that fundamentally shift our conversations about what literature and culture are, or are for. These events create not only ruptures but also possibilities for emergence and thus for different ways of knowing, different understandings of community, as well as different subjects who bring disruptive knowledges with them. Most importantly, emergent events do not have an end point. The point is not a utopian arrival at a transformed world, but a constant shifting of the ground upon which we—writers, critics, publishers, readers, teachers—are standing.

Community—its possibilities and its limitations—is also central to Erika Thorkelson's essay, as she thinks about how and why we fail to communicate across divides of status and generation. Certainly the generational divide has been an important dimension to the CanLit controversies of the past few years. As author Zoe Whittall has pointed out, recent divides on questions of rape culture have been drawn generationally, a topic that feminists are often reluctant to address.[4] At the same time, as this very collection demonstrates, there are ample opportunities for collaboration and coalition between people from multiple generations, working from within different institutional contexts with varying degrees of power and privilege. Thorkelson brings us back to the question of what writing and reading can do, asking if it might teach us to listen more carefully to people with experiences that are not our own. Listening, she concludes, is going to be crucial to rebuilding literary communities rooted in empathy.

The final piece in this section, and in this book as a whole, is thinking not about empathy but about accountability and how the refusal of CanLit is also a being-accountable to other sorts of communities. As Daniel Heath Justice writes in *Why Indigenous Literatures Matter*, "We are sorely in need of more accountable kindness in our critical work as well as in our relationships."[5] Joshua Whitehead powerfully evokes the failures of accountability that have defined CanLit, and decentres CanLit as a white colonial project in favour of Indigenous Lit. He brings us back to the question of rupture, of what is broken apart, broken open, and what becomes possible from within the wreckage. More vitally still, Whitehead refuses the colonial project of CanLit, and refuses what Leanne Betasamosake Simpson has named as the "mainstreaming" impulse that's made imperative for so many writers. He does not move Cree aside to make way for English. Rather, refusal comes in the form of many gifts: stories, language, memories, communities that may not belong to you, the reader, but are gifted to you by the writer. Here, refusal is generosity. It is situatedness. It is knowledge and it is strength. Here, refusal is power in all its generative possibility.

On Not Refusing CanLit

LAURA MOSS

January 25, 2018

Today a friend of mine said that he gave up on CanLit. Over the course of the last year, with the prevalence of vitriolic conversations in the field and with the exposure of predators in positions of power in creative writing communities, I too have been tempted, repeatedly, to step away.

For some whose relationship to CanLit has been abusive, breaking up is an important, even necessary, act of resistance and reclamation. For me, as an editor and a teacher, I can't walk away. I refuse to give up on Canadian literature. I refuse to read Joseph Boyden or Margaret Atwood as metonymic of CanLit. I refuse to give credence to vile tweets and public condemnation of women I admire in Canadian literary studies.

I want to stand in solidarity and as an ally as best as I can, when my presence is wanted and productive.

I refuse to adhere to a narrow and damaging version of CanLit that hears the voices of some and excludes the voices of many. I pause here to disentangle "CanLit" as a noun synecdoche of all that is broken in the writing industry and the academy from "CanLit" as a short-form term that refers to the history of writing in Canada. I use it as the latter, but for some, especially lately, CanLit is the former. For them, it has come to stand in for something that is exclusive and representative of only a few writers. That is the CanLit of restrictive politics and abusive power whose genealogy extends far beyond its public eruption in the present. That is the CanLit of current dumpster-fire fame and the CanLit from which my friend walked away. I have zero desire to defend such CanLit and I fully respect those who say that version of CanLit does not reflect them.

I acknowledge that CanLit, but can't forget all that has resisted and exceeded it. I do wish, however, that those criticizing CanLit whole-hog would slow down and remember the complex history of writing in Canada. I hope that the recent toxic version of CanLit does not negate the important history of writing and thinking done across the country over centuries—by people across the political spectrum and often by people who had to fight hard to be seen and heard. This is not a celebration of literary history. It is a call to recognize that the incompleteness of Canadian literary culture is not a recent phenomenon. Exclusion and elitism have always been part of CanLit, as has resistance. I want to remember that. Elsewhere I have written about why I stand by the imperfect umbrella of Canadian literature. The main reason has to do with my commitment to remembering the specificities of historical, political, creative, and social contexts in the production and reception of Canadian culture. Contextual knowledge is necessary to remember what has been done in the name of the nation and within the specific laws of the country. Context contains memory, and the spectres of national memory still haunt the present.

I want to read the words of people who fight for breath.

I approach Canadian literature in the context of the university classroom in which I teach the literary history of Canada and within the framework of the academic journal I edit. Over the last twenty years in my CanLit classes, I have taught writing by Jeannette Armstrong, Juliane Okot Bitek, Dionne Brand, Nicole Brossard, Sara Jeannette Duncan, SKY Lee, P.K. Page, Eden Robinson, Laura Goodman Salverson, Mary Ann Shadd, Carol Shields, and Rita Wong, among many others. My CanLit classroom includes conversations about race and gender and class and history and mobility in

Canadian cultural and social contexts. I refuse to give up on these conversations. I teach the histories of experimental poetry, genealogical narratives, historiographic metafiction, dystopias, environmental theatre, and dozens of other forms. We trace intellectual debates and controversies over decades and even centuries in Canada. It is powerful and important.

I want to give students the opportunity to encounter the varied literary voices and traditions of Canada in the space of a university classroom.

I refuse to give up on CanLit because of the student who came up to me after class today to say thank you.[1] For the past two weeks on Monday, Wednesday, and Friday on the way to UBC from Surrey, she has been subjected to racist comments at a construction site she has to pass. It has been relentless, she said. Sitting in a classroom, talking about discourses of legitimacy and illegitimacy in SKY Lee's *Disappearing Moon Cafe* and talking about the long history of racism in Canada, she said she felt empowered. She said she felt like she could assert legitimacy in this space by making her own story legible.

I refuse to foreclose on untold stories.

Every term at the beginning of my Canadian literature class, I ask, *Why study CanLit?* The answers we come up with are also the reasons I can't walk away. I think the students and I need to know the layers of stories of the place we stand. We need to hear from an array of voices and perspectives. We need to trace the histories of censorship and speech, of discrimination and publication, of form and content. We need to know cultural and countercultural history. We need to engage the beauty, humour, and horrors of Canadian literature.

My heart is too heavy to give up on CanLit. I refuse.

Visions and Versions of Resilience
Mentoring as a Means of Survival

PHOEBE WANG

In times of grief and disclosure, when stories we have always lived beside like weather precipitate in the air like a sudden storm, stories of abuses of power and of silencing, in such times I look not for ways to allay that grief, but to survive it. In seeking for ways to survive, I have seen how we learn from survivors and from those who have resisted, and not from those who have historically held power, or those who could believe in the myths that Canadians tell about themselves. Consequently, those who benefit most from these liberal myths and who can live without questioning the facade of equality and multiculturalism are, in fact, the least resilient, while those who have had their experiences and expertise dismissed, whose stories have been ignored or silenced, and whose lives have been unvalued are ultimately our strongest champions, elders and teachers and mentors. From generation to generation, we ask the most from those who have survived the most. In a sense, being mentored and mentoring are themselves acts of resilience and survival.

Mentoring forges a lineage outside of kinship ties. While in other professions, choosing a mentor is a matter of finding someone who has expertise and experience, in creative disciplines, it links up practitioners of a shared craft and way of being in the world. It spills beyond the confines of a strictly professional relationship. It creates inheritors and, in some ways, a tenuous, impalpable practice to be inherited. These lines of inheritance are often invisible, traceable only through public thanks and acknowledgements pages. More and more, finding a creative writing mentor has become the purview of institutions and graduate programs rather than the organic outcome of circumstance and community.

When I was in my twenties and starting to feel the shape of my writing practice, I longed to know not only the intricacies of my craft, but also how to sustain a writing life. How to keep it alive when it almost spluttered out like a spark on wet leaves. It didn't occur to me that mentors and elders might exist to answer the questions I didn't know to ask. If I met my twenty-year-old self now, I would see a young woman who was more in need of models and mentoring than most. I would tell her that she did not need to fit herself or her imagination into a tradition or formal constraints, that there were few precedents for the kind of life she would occupy, and that she must write into the very split of her difference. I see now, with the perspective of fifteen years, that others might have failed in some capacity to recognize what I needed.

It's painful to recall how little I understood my needs as a writer of colour. Yet I was extremely fortunate; my parents were artistic, hard-working, and with enough energy to adapt themselves in a new country. They were also immigrants, isolated, financially insecure, and confronting the effects of their own emotional neglect and physical abuse. As a family, we were fiercely self-reliant, but then we had to be. The mantra of hard work and independence is symptomatic of many immigrants and newcomers to Canada, further exacerbated by a lack of knowledge of the resources available and a distaste for asking too much from our host country. As a result, those most needing of tangible supports are usually those the least willing to ask for them.

By the time my family relocated to Vancouver and I was at UBC, my uncomplaining, self-denying mindset of the "good guest" was yielding to the pressures of all that was unacknowledged. Now that I work for an institution,

I see how profoundly first-generation, immigrant and international students, and students of colour are disoriented by the disconjunct between the pervading discourse of diversity and the meagre acknowledgement of the real barriers they face. The effects of intergenerational trauma, cultural differences and the pressure to succeed academically results in these students being particularly prone to mental health issues. Even as someone who was born in Canada, my sense of alienation was so acute that near the end of my degree I couldn't read or write. I never finished my honours thesis, leaving my degree uncompleted for years and my poetry strangling itself under the weight of what it could not disclose.

I did not have a mentor until I was thirty, when I entered the U of T Creative Writing MA program. We chose mentors or had mentors chosen for us on the basis of genre or of shared stylistic qualities, as well as on the basis of their reputation and prestige. We hoped for tangible results, feedback on our work, introductions to editors and agents, recommendation letters, and, of course, advice on how or where to publish. What we really needed were mentors who could teach us to be resilient, to survive, to weather financial precarity, the granting system, agents, publishing contracts, and book tours while still fuelling a creative practice. We needed mentors who could show us our own privilege and challenge our biases, who would help us cope with jealousy and rejection and disappointment, who were models of how to create and nurture community, how to be generous teachers in turn. Do such mentors exist? Would they have materialized, had I called upon them?

I would like to put forth a version and vision of mentorship that may upset the sanctified notion that the writing workshop should focus only on craft and not on identity politics. Yet to deny that writers of colour have needs above and beyond those of white-identifying students would invalidate the lived experience from which writers draw to generate creative works, and the historical and ongoing inequities which BIPOC students of writing will encounter in their careers. It is not enough for creative writing programs to simply value the lives, experiences and stories of all its students or to merely attempt to attract, admit, and offer equal supports to students from as wide a range of backgrounds as possible. Additional supports and resources are necessary, such as faculty and mentors of colour, anti-racism and harassment workshops, and cultural competency training for both faculty and students. Ideally, I would also want to see scholarships and financial support for those students whose communities and families have been historically oppressed, who have survived atrocities such as residential schools, enslavement, and human trafficking. I would like to see resources allocated and counselling support made available for those students who are undergoing the effects of intergenerational trauma. Even if the money and resources are not available, there could be the acknowledgement that writers who have experienced discrimination and marginalization will navigate their careers, and indeed their creative processes, differently. Such an acknowledgement would go a long way toward creating a less opaque and alienating atmosphere within the institution.

The atmosphere of Canadian publishing, especially in the hub of Toronto, may appear to be stylistically varied and eager for new audiences. There are many who are welcoming and who are generous with their time and attention. Yet at the same time, there's also a sense of secrecy and buried histories, of a "whisper network," an inexplicable feeling of "this is how things have always been done," and a need for newcomers to conform to unspoken rules rather than the industry finding ways to translate and clarify its expectations, particularly to those who are cultural outsiders, who are not well-versed in Canadian social customs, or who are non-native speakers of English. This is counterintuitive, given the industry's push toward diversity and inclusion. I can only surmise that it wants to publish those diverse writers who are already familiar with the industry's tacit practices and are ready to conform to them.

During the program and in the years afterwards, my friends and classmates congregated at each other's houses, where conversation would inevitably slide to the coterie of male editors and critics and the influence they held. We bemoaned the latest piece of critical claptrap published in some national forum, the predictable choices they made when soliciting work, and so on and so forth until the bottles were empty, the sun had set, and nothing had been solved. At that time, our conversations had a predictable arc. Because of our innate belief that the status quo would never change, we did not talk about solutions. It occurred to me that this mindset, in fact, would solidify the status quo; by giving these editors and critics such importance in our conversations, we allowed them to take space that might otherwise be generative. In giving relevance to these self-appointed critics and "gatekeepers," we made them and their work relevant, made them clickbait. I realized suddenly that even emerging writers, with little reputation or sway, could have power through our refusal to engage. We could invest our attention elsewhere and imagine other spaces, where there would be room for the conversations we wanted to have, and this became a means to thrive.

Amongst writers of colour, and Asian-Canadian writers particularly, the lack of mentors is possibly one of the greatest barriers we experience. Those mentors we have are only one-generation deep and so have had to be both the driving wedge as well as the foundation for the next generation, and often they are weary from the years of activism and, movingly, a misplaced sense of failure, of not doing enough. Since their publications have only recently become included in the Canadian literary canon, and since the decades of Asian-Canadians' resistance and redress work is rarely taught in literature or history courses, I myself had little knowledge of the works of Roy Miki, Fred Wah, SKY Lee, Jim Wong-Chu, Lydia Kwa, Larissa Lai, Rita Wong, and many others. It was not until I grew weary of the canonical whiteness of my English degree that I found courses on what were at the time termed "minority literatures." When I was able to meet the writers of colour I read and admired, many of them expressed how often they had been promised by well-meaning institutions, organizations, and publications that real change was forthcoming, only to once again be disappointed by the lack of action and the rhetorical lip service of diversity and inclusion. They were now looking for change to come from the next generation, yet those who are being loaded with this undertaking lack the institutional memory of previous cohorts of writers and activists who founded associations, collectives, magazines, and presses and worked in various reconciliation and redress movements. Without connecting emerging writers of colour to older mentors who have also experienced racism and marginalization and who can pass on ways of resistance and of resilience, we risk fighting over the same fraught ground over and over again, with each cohort having to repeatedly struggle for recognition and justify their fundamental rights and freedoms, even their very lives.

This is not to say this upcoming generation of writers of colour can necessarily follow the same models as previous generations or use the same strategies and tactics for destabilizing the status quo. Factors such as demographics, class, and colonialism impact the role of mentoring each generation of writers. As a first-generation Canadian, I grew up among other working-class Chinese children of grocery store and laundromat owners. We spoke English at school and Cantonese at home, and were inured to the idea that certain positions and opportunities would still be barred from us. This line of thinking may appear to be self-defeating passivity, equally difficult to explain and to root out. I am constantly finding it like tumours in myself, tied up with the entrenched idea that I ought to be grateful for what I have. A cursory count of the numbers of people of colour who have published books, who are editors, agents, and publishers, who work in publishing, who are directors of festivals and organizations makes me see that I should be asking for much more.

This up-and-coming generation of Asian-Canadian writers are experiencing similar yet distinct challenges. For one thing, *Asian-Canadian* may not even be an accurate term to describe them. As a result of the surging rise of the middle class in countries such as China, Korea, and Singapore and the value placed on Western education, more and more international students are recent arrivals in Canada and do not yet see themselves as Asian-Canadian, even if they graduate in Canada and go on to write, publish, and work here. They may have relatively more financial stability than previous generations of immigrants, but they are also more isolated and lack support networks. Coming from countries where they are a part of the majority, they may be less weighed by the experiences of discrimination that have marked all people of colour in Canada, yet they may also be unaware of the more insidious forms of racism in Canadian cultural industries and institutions. I continue to struggle with connecting them to older members of the community, and with empowering younger writers, without transmitting feelings of disillusionment that inevitably accompany a deeper understanding of the Canadian literary scene.

This shortage of mentors and faculty of colour has resulted in many Black, Muslim, Indigenous, Asian and South Asian first-time authors finding ourselves, often at a relatively young age, doing work that resembles mentoring. On many occasions, friends of mine were impressed when a young person found me in the crowd, excitedly asking if I was Phoebe Wang. There was no doubt I was Phoebe Wang. There were no other Asian people at the event. I myself had found many writers of colour the same way. Something interesting would happen at events whenever more than one of us was there at the same time. One of us was a signal of diversity at work. Two of us, solidarity. Three? Practically a revolution. If there were three of us together, chatting, complaining, and plotting together, people in the room would send us glances. The air around us seemed to shift and charge with meaning. The whiteness of the room was no longer opaque. Despite my own discomfort with being present and visible at literary events, with maintaining a blog and a presence on social media, these forms of engagement serve an important purpose—but one with internal contradictions. The presence of people of colour can be a disruption and yet also give the veneer of diversity. It can be viewed as sociability and self-promotion and also as selflessness and community building. Emerging BIPOC writers can find us in an overwhelmingly white crowd, but our attendance can be read as a validation of the alienating and toxic dynamic of the event, the conference, and the writing workshop.

I question whether I have the wisdom to mentor others, but I feel as though I have little choice. The need is too great. So I plunge ahead, possibly giving perspectives that are too subjective and limited, dispensing advice that is too cautious, prioritizing unfruitful projects or spending out too much of my emotional investment, caring too much, worrying too much. For instance, in years past I would explain to younger writers the necessity of attending events, how to navigate predatory or inebriated writers, when my time would have better been spent on lobbying publishers and editors to hold events in spaces that were more safe, welcoming, and accessible.

My own visibility contrasts with the invisibility of my mentoring work, which includes sharing my own limited knowledge about contracts, grants, publishing, publicity, and book tours. It is voluntary labour but it is also sharing, connecting, and giving friendship. It is a reciprocal relationship and I would almost prefer for it to be unacknowledged, except for amongst my community, in case it somehow irks or angers those who believe I'm giving preference to writers on the basis of racialized identities. More than once I have had to justify why a space or a meeting is open only to those who self-identify as BIPOC and I will probably have to continue to do so. Meanwhile I will be actively reading, tracking, and meeting emerging writers of colour to the best of my ability, so that I can do for them what came so late for me: passing on their work to publishers and editors who have indicated they want to publish more writers of colour, introducing them to event organizers desirous of being more inclusive in their programming, and seeing that their books are reviewed and received by as wide an audience as possible. Yet, going forward from this historical moment of the #MeToo movement and the failure of our creative writing programs and publishers to support women, I also want to imagine my mentorship differently. Instead of simply sharing knowledge to build resiliency, I will also be imagining a future in which we can do more than survive. We must change the oppressive and damaging conditions within CanLit that result in painful and traumatic episodes that must be overcome and survived. It begins with not merely passing down stories of survivorship, but the tools for challenging the status quo, for holding different kinds of conversations, and for being in different kinds of spaces. For speaking with our absence and non-attendance when being present would be taken for tacit validation and approval. Because when we are done grieving we will be ready for rebuilding, using shapes we recognize but in an irrefutable arrangement that will outlast what we make alone.

In the "New CanLit," We Must All Be Antigones

A. H. REAUME

One of my favourite plays is Sophocles's *Antigone*. It's about a young woman who is told by her uncle, the king, that she isn't allowed to bury her brother and that anyone who does will be put to death. But rather than listen to what the voice of authority tells her to do, Antigone does what she thinks is right—at great personal cost.

Antigone has always epitomized courage for me. To stand up to those in power and do what you believe to be just is a frightening thing. But it's also a necessary one.

Change often happens when those on the margins challenge those who hold power. But challenging power isn't easy. No one really *wants* to do it. Working for change is a thankless job. It sucks up all your time. It often involves saying the same things over and over again to people who refuse to listen, and who then say that you're too aggressive, or too confrontational, or too much of whatever other insult they think will shut you up.

If you become an activist, you will have uncomfortable confrontations with people you admire. You'll lose friends. It will likely harm your career. It will almost certainly burn you out and leave you mentally exhausted.

So, why do people do it? Activists are often people who don't have a choice—they either speak up or they lose. Often they lose anyways. This is the unfair burden that injustice places on those who are marginalized. Not only do they have to cope with the violence of their own marginalization, but they also have to carry the burden of fighting against that marginalization. And while those with more privilege sometimes add their voices to the fight, this happens far less often than it should.

CanLit is a field in which many marginalized people have spent their lives losing and losing again. Marsha Lederman, in her *Globe and Mail* article "Twitterature: Wading into the Choppy Waters of CanLit,"[1] evokes a nostalgic pre-UBCAccountable CanLit filled with "prairie landscapes, the immigrant experience or gentle but pithy observations about the Two Solitudes"; but that serenity was achieved, in part, by excluding voices. You can't have a disagreement if one person has a major book deal with a multinational and a dozen festival spots and the other has a book out from a small press that no one has bothered to review because mainstream review culture didn't believe more "diverse" stories deserved attention. Go back before the 1960s and publishing was even more exclusionary because there weren't independent Canadian presses boosting the voices of these authors.

How have marginalized writers been silenced in CanLit? To start with, marginalized people have often been told explicitly or in so many words by publishers and lit magazines that their stories aren't "universal" enough. If the magazine or publisher was trying to publish more "diverse" stories, they might instead have been told that their story wasn't "diverse" in the right way.

This has led some to, understandably, engage in self-silencing. Writer Alicia Elliott explains it best in an interview with *Room* magazine:[2] "I wasn't writing for Indigenous readers because the gatekeepers who are publishing are not Indigenous and I had to make sure this was appealing to them."

Even the more diverse books that have been published in recent years have faced barriers. But how does one even quantify those barriers? In CanLit, oppression doesn't always take the form of outright discriminatory comments or actions—it often comes in the form of what's called "unconscious" or structural discrimination. After all, how can you really tell if you were passed up for a literary prize because your book wasn't good enough or because the all-white or male or non-Indigenous or straight or able-bodied jury was unconsciously biased toward stories that were more "relatable" (read: white, cis, heterosexual, male, and able-bodied).

This could be seen at play when judges during Canada Reads 2018[3] said that Cherie Dimaline's *The Marrow Thieves*, a dystopian book that addresses the colonial oppression of Indigenous people, wasn't real enough or that it wasn't as relevant as other books since it was more important for people to "work on themselves" than change the world. It was a telling glimpse into the arguments that might dismiss books by marginalized writers in other competitions.

Perhaps one of the benefits of the recent CanLit controversies is that they have surfaced truths about CanLit that used to be quietly talked about behind closed doors. For years, I've heard stories of publishers telling women of colour they couldn't publish their books because they didn't fit stereotypical narratives about race or gender and so wouldn't sell. I've heard of agents unwilling to represent books with queer or transgender themes. I once witnessed four people make racist comments to a Chinese-Canadian friend during the twenty minutes we spent at a networking event at the Canadian Writers' Summit. And I also heard many whispers about male writers and rumours of them harassing or assaulting female writers.

When the UBCAccountable letter was published, or the "Appropriation Prize" was suggested, these were just the straws that broke the metaphorical camel's back. People were outraged by these stories, but their anger was also rooted in the long history behind the headlines.

I vividly remember reading UBCAccountable's letter for the first time. I was brought back to my time as a student at UBC. In 2006, I was the founding editor of *Antigone Magazine*, a feminist magazine that encouraged women to get into leadership, politics, and activism. In that capacity, young women came to me with stories of the assault and sexual harassment they experienced through their involvement in party politics—but also at the hands of professors.

After reading the UBCAccountable letter, I thought of those young women I had spent so much time speaking with and of the survivors of all ages across

CanLit who were terrified of speaking out. No woman who comes forward to allege a violation of this kind should have to deal with prominent authors writing a letter that seemed, to many of the young writers I'm friends with, to be in support of the man they accused of violating them.

Like many writers, I spoke out to encourage signatories to take their names off UBCAccountable. Since UBCAccountable, I have heard many stories about women afraid to make accusations against other men in CanLit because they fear that something similar will happen to them. There's a reason why anonymous emails are being sent to publishers about people on their staff, and students at Concordia are staging protests to get the university to take their complaints seriously.

But while many in CanLit have looked the other way or resolutely kept their names on the UBCAccountable letter, a community of those who have called these writers out, or spoken up on issues related to the Appropriation Prize, has formed. This community, connected by Facebook and Twitter, has been called the "New CanLit" by people like author Jen Sookfong Lee.[4] I am heartened by the many writers who have shown support for writers who experience harassment or assault—people like Lawrence Hill, Zoe Whittall, Jen Sookong Lee, Dorothy Ellen Palmer, Keith Maillard, Alicia Elliott, and too many others to name. Similarly, more Indigenous writers and writers of colour have been given broader platforms to articulate the challenges they face, including Gwen Benaway, Daniel Heath Justice, Joshua Whitehead, Kateri Akiwenzie-Damm, Natalie Wee, Jael Richardson, and Carrianne Leung.

This support and resistance might tempt some to declare that the post-UBCAccountable and Appropriation Prize era might not be something solely to be lamented. Many people have questioned whether, just as a forest fire can bring forth new and necessary life, the various dumpster fires that Alicia Elliott identified in her iconic piece, "CanLit Is a Raging Dumpster Fire,"[5] can potentially engender something better. Are these fertile ruins?

The spring 2017 issue *Canadian Literature* would urge us to be cautious in our predictions—-and also our use of forest-fire metaphors, with Laura

Moss and Brendan McCormack writing, "We might talk about how wildfires are natural and regenerative but that would provide little comfort to someone standing, staring at the remains of their burnt home and community. They would likely be uninterested in having their losses read metaphorically, let alone optimistically."[6]

The danger of this move to optimism is something Jael Richardson articulated during the GritLit panel she shared in Hamilton with Alicia Elliott and Carrianne Leung, *CanLit REALLY is a Raging Dumpster Fire*. This panel was created after an earlier panel—"Is CanLit a Raging Dumpster Fire?"—was cancelled for centring white voices while directly citing Elliott's words in the title.[7] During the panel, Richardson stated: "People expect you to move into hope quicker than you're ready. People who aren't fighting want to be more hopeful because they don't want to get involved—they don't want to get in the trenches themselves."[8]

Richardson, Elliott, and Leung also reminded attendees that the dumpster fires are still raging and there hasn't been any systemic change to put them out.[9]

That's why the rhetoric of hope is dangerous. It threatens to silence the movement for change by covering over CanLit's continuing systemic inequalities with a veneer of superficial progress. It asks people who have been starved for years to be satisfied with being thrown a bone—one that someone else has already picked over.

This movement toward hope was rightly called by many a tactic of white feminism.[10] [11] It's an attempt to deny the lingering inequalities that exist for BIPOCs, queer, trans, and disabled people by people who either don't see those inequalities because of their privilege or don't want to see them.

It appears to be the same philosophy behind attempts by both Margaret Atwood and Susan Swan to, as Swan said in a tweet,[12] negotiate a resolution after UBCAccountable—despite the fact that the half-hearted apology they later released showed that neither seemed to want to take true accountability for the harm they caused. This can also be seen in their donations to help women who have been assaulted—where they are fixated on "due process" rather than justice for victims. In coverage of the fund, Atwood has emphasized that women who don't "properly report inappropriate behavior with evidence and documentation" can "alienate a lot of people from feminism."[13]

Moss and McCormack remind us of the persistence of the status quo: "The hegemony of the 'old growth' is resilient because it re-seeds itself even while it is being put to flame. Hence, we witness dialectical cycles of burning, growing, burning, growing, but perhaps less systemic or structural transformation as might be anticipated because of the power of power to replicate itself."[14]

This status quo is also being reproduced within the New CanLit. Just because someone has been an ally on UBCAccountable issues doesn't mean they're willing to be an ally on other issues. White privilege is often what gets in the way. But so does ableist privilege, and heterosexual privilege, and cis privilege, and class privilege, and all the other ways some of us have more power than others.

It's not surprising that many fighting for change are burning out or taking temporary steps back. That's part of the heartbreaking nature of activism—it is almost always slow, iterative, disappointing, and punishing. Power very rarely yields in the revolutionary ways that are necessary. Usually, you take a step forward and then promptly need to brace for backlash. Because of that, activists are often consumed, just like Antigone was, by the back-breaking struggle against the refusal of power to bend.

But the activists of the New CanLit have something Antigone did not. We have each other. The sense of community in this New CanLit has greatly moved me, even while it has sometimes disappointed me. Whether it is people taking turns holding UBCAccountable accountable, or writers like Elaine Corden helping to start the hashtag #settlercollector[15] on Twitter to take on some of the burden of anti-Indigenous trolling after the Colten Boushie and Tina Fontaine verdicts, there is a heartening sense of communal responsibility and care.

But if we are to have a chance of uprooting the Old Growth of CanLit, we must do as Carrianne Leung advised in the GritLit panel when she said, "I would like to shift us from hope to justice."[16]

In activist communities, there is a very specific history behind the shift to justice-based activism. Equality-based disability activism, for example, was about working for rights and access. In contrast, justice-based activism is focused on dismantling the idea that being able-bodied is inherently better.

It is also a framework that disability justice activist Mia Mingus explains is working toward "building an understanding of disability that is more complex, whole and interconnected than what we have previously found. We are disabled people who are people of color; women, genderqueer and transgender; poor and working class; youth; immigrants; lesbian, gay, bisexual and queer; and more."[17] If we are to create a better CanLit, it must be one built on a similar idea of justice.

This won't be easy. CanLit is, at heart, an industry. But there are still ways in which we can work within the "CanLit Industrial Complex" to make space for others and encourage structural change.

We can do this by buying the books of marginalized writers, providing resources to support those with multiple intersections, hiring diverse editors and agents, creating inclusive panels and reading series, starting and supporting festivals celebrating diverse voices like Growing Room and The FOLD, refusing to attend inaccessible events, and building creative writing programs that nurture marginalized writers and protect students.

We also need to reject the system that centralizes power and prestige, festivals and reviews in the hands of a few people and create a more equitable vision for Canadian literature.

It's critical, too, for writers to consider the ways in which our privilege plays into our activism. To think about how it affects when we speak up and when we stay silent. If we are called out for our privilege, we must learn how to put our feelings aside and change.

If we want to work toward justice, we need to realize that our feelings aren't sacred. What is sacred is the difficult but necessary work of building community across differences. We won't always do this perfectly, but we owe it to our fellow writers to do it better and to take responsibility for educating ourselves.

I believe the New CanLit needs all of us to be Antigones—people who challenge the status quo and work for justice even at personal cost. The only way we can force CanLit to bend and break and reshape itself is if more of us take up this role—especially those of us who are relatively privileged. We can't leave the heavy lifting solely to the most marginalized among us. We are all responsible for working for justice.

Fighting for change isn't a sprint, but it also doesn't have to be a marathon. If there are enough of us, it can be a relay race. So, if you've been running for a while, it's okay to take a break. And if you've been sitting on the sidelines, it is your turn.

Reach your hand out—the torch is waiting.

Refusing the Borders of CanLit

JENNIFER ANDREWS

"refuse": to reject or resist (instruction, advice, etc.); to decline to accept or submit to (a command, rule, decision, penalty, etc.).

—OED online

The Canada-US border has been described as the longest undefended border in the world. In the post-9/11 era, crossing the border at an official port of entry even as a white cisgendered heterosexual women with Canadian citizenship involves preparation: up-to-date government-issued photo identification, detailed information on the reason for and destination of the visit, and clear assurances that I am not going to benefit monetarily from attending a conference or visiting an archive. Invariably when I am asked what I do for a living, I end up explaining that I am an English professor and that I study CanLit. You'd be surprised how many border guards—Canadian and American—take delight in testing my knowledge or asking for book recommendations. My visible privilege makes the process of border-crossing easy. Nor am I ever questioned about whether I will return to Canada, or whether I am welcome back into Canada. The borders are clear—and for those border guards I belong north of the 49th parallel.

The gatekeeping one encounters at a border crossing appears, for those who are deemed to belong, a benign and even reassuring process, ensuring that those who are perceived to threaten the safety of the nation are identified and kept out. Academia, strange as it may sound, is not much different. University institutions are dedicated, ostensibly, to opening the minds of students to new ideas and educating them for the future; but just as readily, there is a process of filtering that occurs in post-secondary institutions that depends upon surveying, patrolling, and reinforcing borders, particularly those that define disciplines and specific fields of study. And in English, at least, those fields of study are usually all too often determined by the author's use of the English language and the recognition of national borders.

While English literary studies may appear to be a foundational discipline, it is, in fact, a relatively recent addition to degree-granting institutions, dating back to the nineteenth century. Courses in American literature were first offered in 1828, only to be halted in 1830 by the reassertion of Ivy League institutions that Greek and Latin should prevail; despite this, American literature did grow as a legitimate field of study in the late nineteenth century south and north of the Canada-US border. Conversely, the teaching of CanLit courses at universities is a much newer phenomenon that first emerged in the latter half of the twentieth-century as part of the country's efforts to recognize White, Western, Anglophone Canadian culture as worthy of study and a significant part of the training of a nation's citizens.

My professors of Canadian literature at McGill, where I completed my undergraduate degree (1989 to 1993), and the University of Toronto, where I undertook my MA and PhD (1993 to 1998), were part of a first wave of individuals who had had the opportunity to study Canadian writing and claim their expertise in the area not merely as a digression from more established areas of literary study. To create new fields of study—national or otherwise—is difficult, requiring a boldness of purpose and an unwavering focus, particularly when one's subject of study is located right beside the largest superpower in the world. So while American radio, television, movies, and goods streamed into Canada during my childhood, teen, and university years, the post-Centennial era prompted governments to invest much more heavily in the creation and support of Canadian culture as unique and worthy of public and scholarly attention.

By the time I completed my honours degree in English in 1993, Canadian literature had become a regularly advertised field of study in English departments across Canada. I had also spent a semester studying American literature at Duke University in North Carolina and was fascinated by the ways in which the two countries seemed so very similar yet so incredibly different. Knowing I was entering a job market where there might only be one or two academic posts in a year (if I was lucky), I strategically decided to improve my odds and wrote a PhD thesis that offered a comparative view of nineteenth- and twentieth-century English-Canadian and American literature. That way, I could apply not only for the very limited number of Canadian literature jobs, usually housed only at Canadian institutions, but also look south of the border to American universities to broaden my search. I have been warned never to play poker because my face is too expressive; nonetheless, I took great pride in my ability to gamble with my job prospects by improving the odds. What I had not anticipated was that in shoring up the borders of CanLit to ensure its rightful place in the academy, I might be perceived of as an illegitimate offspring or an intruder, potentially destined to be denied entry.

The rigid nature of borders became crystal clear during my first on-campus job interview for a coveted tenure-track English-Canadian literature position at a large western Canadian research university as I was finishing my doctorate. For most people, a job interview may last a couple of hours, or perhaps at most a day; it can involve standardized testing, answering the questions of a group or individuals, touring a company's office, and perhaps sharing a meal with staff. In academia, the process is far more complex, mostly because a permanent tenure-track post means sharing the water cooler with someone potentially for an entire career. The process usually involves a one- or two-day jam-packed schedule of meetings with deans, chairs, students, faculty, and staff, a formal presentation by the candidate on current research interests, as well as the requisite committee interview and several meals with various people involved in making a final decision.

Candidates are also often asked to teach a class, while being observed. Preparing for an academic interview is time-consuming and intense; there is often little warning given to candidates, and the reality of working around a committee's schedule means being flexible and ready to respond to any question at a moment's notice. And yet, despite all of that work, there is no guarantee that you will be hired; nor is there much information provided for those who do not get an offer. For instance, my first experience was flavoured with dismissiveness and even open hostility for a whole host of reasons I will never fully understand. Maybe I seemed too privileged to understand life in a working-class western Canadian city. I am a central Canadian—born and raised in Toronto—a fact that was referenced multiple times by the hiring committee. Perhaps it was my youthful naiveté. I was twenty-six at the time, a baby in academia where the average age of a PhD graduate in all fields of study is thirty-six. But what I did not predict was how my decision to write a comparative English-Canadian and American literature thesis would be regarded by the gatekeepers of CanLit.

As part of my interview, I was asked to deliver the requisite "job talk," a.k.a. a potted description of my doctoral dissertation to an audience of potential colleagues, graduate students trying to gather intel on this mysterious process, and an occasional enthusiastic undergraduate student. Make no mistake: those who attend are there to test the candidate, so finding common ground while impressing the audience is crucial—boring them is not okay. My doctoral work focused on humour in nineteenth- and twentieth-century English-Canadian and American literature, a topic that is invariably unfunny. Trying to unpack the motivations of a joke in theoretical terms guarantees failure. So in an effort to match my talk to the job description, which required expertise in twentieth-century Canadian literature, and to establish a rapport with the audience, I presented an analysis of Thomas King's well-known novel, *Green Grass, Running Water*. Nominated for the Governor-General's Literary Award for fiction in 1993 and prominent on national and international bestseller lists, King's book would likely be familiar to my audience. Set in a contemporary Blackfoot community in Alberta, the novel combines scatological humour with a satirical examination of the imposition of Judeo-Christian and white Western beliefs on Indigenous communities through multiple playful retellings of an origin story that defies and subverts traditional Christian narratives. Most importantly, the novel is laugh-out-loud funny, offering a perfect vehicle for what might otherwise be perceived as an overly dry and theoretical talk.

Looking back, my choice to focus on King was provocative at the time, and deliberately so. King is an American-born Cherokee writer who lives and works in Canada and has spent much of his career writing about the complexities of the Canada-US border. As he argues in a now-famous line from a 1990 interview with Constance Rooke: "I guess I'm supposed to believe in a line that exists between the US and Canada, but for me it is an imaginary line. It's a line from someone else's imagination" (72). His observations about the Canadian-American border had challenged me as a privileged white Canadian to think differently about nation-state impositions, and I was excited by that. While the job talk was initially well-received, my enthusiasm turned to shock and confusion when I was queried about my literary and national loyalties, given my interest in border-crossing scholarship. For those faculty members who had invested their careers in the study of CanLit and likely could remember a time when CanLit was regarded as unworthy of institutional recognition or investment, my stance was fundamentally disconcerting and potentially threatening.

Academic job postings in literature even today rely heavily on national borders to articulate specific fields of study. Ads often begin with keywords that literally delineate the borders of the field using nation-states, and then narrow their focus by referencing a specific time period and often a particular genre; smaller departments may omit such details, because of the breadth of teaching needs required. For example, an ad posted by Acadia University in October 2017 asks for an "Assistant Professor of Canadian literature and theory," whereas larger-sized universities with graduate programs will provide specifics, referencing both particular periods of coverage (usually the nineteenth or twentieth century) and genre, to ensure that the department has sufficient coverage to supervise master's and doctoral students interested in poetry rather than, say, fiction. In this case, the job I was interviewing for was twentieth-century Canadian literature, though I cannot twenty years later recall if there was a specific genre of expertise requested. Having written a comparative thesis, I presumed, would enable access to opportunities on both sides of the forty-ninth parallel. But I soon learned that my Gumby-like flexibility was perceived as a liability rather than an asset. In other words, the securing of borders matters even in a university classroom. The post-interview question period soon devolved as audience members pointedly asked if I was really a Canadianist or just a wannabe Canadianist, feigning interest in Canadian texts but ultimately loyal to an American point of view. The implication was that, if I were to be hired to teach and study English-Canadian literature, the department needed to be sure that I would fit the box it had ticked in initiating a hiring for this specific position and that my commitment to the area was sound. Canada may have been, at that moment, the longest undefended border in the world, but CanLit had its own border guards and I was not passing their scrutiny.

Paradoxically, I encountered a similar situation at the MLA eight months later, when interviewing for a job in American poetry at another prominent western Canadian research institution. This was my second encounter with the job posting, having been long- and short-listed for the same job the previous year, a search that ended in failure when the university cancelled the hire days before I was scheduled to fly out for an on-campus interview. To be clear, my thesis was on prose—not poetry—but I had begun research for a post-doctoral project on contemporary Native North American women's poetry, prompted by King's arguments to explore Indigenous poets on both sides of the forty-ninth parallel. I was a savvier candidate that second time around and deliberately asked about border-crossing possibilities. I was emphatically told the job required remaining focused on the national field being advertised: commit to American poetry or take a hike. I breathed a sigh of relief when I was not short-listed for the job, knowing I would be miserable confined to a specific national field and genre for life, when the research I was conducting fundamentally overturned the nation-state borders I viewed as imposed and in need of rethinking.

Physical borders are one thing. Academic borders are another. Oddly enough, they share many of the same characteristics and are all too often rigorously policed by those who have the most to lose were they to disappear. For scholars who have spent their lives legitimizing a specific field of study, creating course offerings, recruiting students, and ultimately producing graduate students who through their appointments at post-secondary institutions can continue this replication. But we live in a settler-colonial nation, one that cannot ignore its historical and contemporary dispossession of Indigenous peoples from their homeland, and the reality that these same tribal communities occupied spaces that straddle the Canada-US border long before our arrival. To ignore how and why borders have been imposed is to overlook a fundamental part of Canada's creation as a nation and dismiss the effects of this kind of regulation, containment, and exclusion, whether at a border crossing or in a university department.

Looking back, I realize that no hiring committee can dictate the terms of a scholar's career. But they can circumscribe a particular vision of what a department member's obligations are in contributing to curriculum development and teaching, conducting research, and undertaking service, at least until that person is established in the department and has tenure. Department cultures vary, but when a tenure-track appointment is made, colleagues understand that hiring an individual likely involves a lifelong commitment, so getting a person that fits with the department's ethos is critical, and that often means not hiring the candidate who makes colleagues uncomfortable, challenges their beliefs, or brings new ideas about curriculum or scholarship. No wonder academic spaces remained dominated by sameness.

To be clear, I became one of the privileged and, as I see it, I was extremely lucky to land where I did. I got a tenure-track job in Canadian literature, albeit in a smaller department where my desire to teach in multiple fields — not just Canadian — was regarded as a bonus and my scholarship on border-crossing Indigenous writers was received with enthusiasm and an eagerness to see those writers incorporated into syllabi. The University of New Brunswick not only has an auspicious history of coupling Canadian literary scholarship and creative writing through journal publications (*The Fiddlehead*, founded at UNB in 1945, and *Studies in Canadian Literature*, which began in 1975), but it was also one of the first university English departments in Canada to cultivate expertise in what was then known as Commonwealth and later postcolonial studies in the late 1960s, recognizing the need to create innovative programs to differentiate themselves from larger Canadian institutions with more clout.

By moving to Fredericton, New Brunswick, I also found myself in a part of Canada that had been struggling with economic and political marginality long before I arrived. While Atlantic Canada is disenfranchised from central Canada, regarded as a "have-not" province in need of federal life-support, the region needs to be understood as far more complex, with its own long-standing contradictions. Fredericton is the provincial capital, situated on the Saint John River and lined on the south side with beautiful historic homes, with the university located literally on top of a hill. Yet the city is a site of deep racial and class prejudices, exemplified by the river that divides it in two. On the north side is the St. Mary's reserve of the Wolastoqiyik people, though to confine the Wolastoqiyik to a single location would be erroneous; the tribe straddles the Canada-US border, from Maine to New Brunswick and Quebec. The north side of the river also includes an area called Barker's Point, historically populated by working-class African-Canadians. The marginality of these residents is portrayed in George Elliott Clarke's *Execution Poems* and *George and Rue*, texts I teach regularly, in which Clarke examines the racism faced by his two Black and Mi'kmaq cousins who robbed and murdered a local Acadian taxi driver with a hammer in Barker's Point, leading to the area's nickname of "Hammer Town," which remains in use today. The cousins were hanged as a result of their crimes, marking the last public execution in Fredericton. But the history of the city's internal divisiveness does not end there. The north side of Fredericton was originally the Acadian village of Sainte-Anne, burned to the ground during the Acadian expulsion and reborn in the nineteenth century as Marysville by New Brunswick lumber, railway, and cotton baron Alexander Gibson, who built a model village for his lumber-mill workers and their families that is still standing; today, the mill houses provincial government offices. But Gibson's story—he ultimately went bankrupt—also represents the decline of Atlantic Canadian prosperity and the shift to a metropolitan centre. The result, as Herb Wyile so persuasively argues in *Anne of Tim Hortons*, is that Atlantic Canada is often regarded by others as "an inconvenient vestige of Confederation, as a fiscal drain on the rest of the country, and as a leisure space" (2). However, for me, as an interloper, it also offered opportunities to deviate from my experiences living in central Canada and to think about the policing of borders within and beyond the nation-state in a whole variety of different ways.

The reality of being a new member of the smallest PhD-granting English department in the country is that you are guaranteed autonomy: institutional borders be damned. Unlike larger institutions with sizable faculty numbers within single departments and the ability to correctively monitor and mould new hires, my department was just relieved to have someone full-time and permanent to teach CanLit and whatever other holes might exist—for instance, the lack of an eighteenth-century British literature specialist from the mid-1990s until 2016, a "gap" of nearly two hundred years of expertise that in a bigger department would have been deemed unacceptable even for a year or so, but one we could limp along without. I was asked by the department chair at my interview if I had any interest in also teaching courses in the eighteenth-century novel (the "doorstopper" course because the books are so thick). While I laughed the query away, it was a pivotal moment in the process because it showed me there was receptivity to movement between and among national fields of study, the very border-crossing that had been ruled out in my interactions with previous institutions during the hiring process.

Although I did not have the pleasure of teaching the eighteenth-century novel course when I first came to UNB, two months after I began as an assistant professor in 1999, I taught my first graduate course, one of my own design that took the established Canadian literary canon to task. In a larger research department, such an opportunity might have occurred after four to five years of teaching, if my work satisfied those patrolling the borders of CanLit. Likewise, the lack of multiple experts in a single field meant there was no one to check my syllabi to ensure that I had "appropriate" coverage or to monitor the content of my courses. It was just assumed that I knew what I was doing, and so I pursued my own border-crossing research and teaching interests—local, tribal, national, and international—in a relatively sheltered and congenial settling, only occasionally bumping up against a lone colleague who questioned whether there was enough Indigenous literature to warrant studying and teaching it (I kid you not). I was confident enough to ignore the provocation and move on, bolstered by the fact that most of my department and my chair were unceasingly supportive and encouraging.

Over the years, I have been able to develop and teach a variety of courses that literally and ideologically straddle the forty-ninth parallel, from a graduate course on the politics of Native North American identities to a special-topics course (designed to recruit students outside the department) on fashion and citizenship that juxtaposes American and Canadian film, television shows, and doll brands. Most recently, as the US elections were taking place in the fall of 2016, I taught a graduate course called Americans Write Canada, which probes how an array of historical and contemporary American authors portray Canada; timed to coincide with the American presidential election, the course was especially meaningful for me and the students, providing unforgettable lessons about the power of borders to include and exclude.

But that autonomy—the seeming flexibility to move across fields of study and to press those borders—comes at a price. Because of my department's relatively small complement in relation to other Canadian English departments, and our ongoing commitments to undergraduate and graduate programming, the opportunity to create a suite of specialized undergraduate courses on topics within CanLit, American literature, or any other field has never really been a practical option, with the exception of special topics, honours, and graduate seminars. Perversely, like the border guards who cannot physically patrol every inch of the Canada-US border, and because of expectations that we ought to provide some knowledge of a variety of fields of study within the increasingly vast field of literary studies, gaps and holes remain. Nor am I ever going to teach in a department where a group of scholars specialize in the same field, a luxury that may enhance camaraderie and collaboration but also allows colleagues to avoid taking responsibility for inclusivity and diversity in their own courses by relying on others or retreating into their own specialized bubbles of authority.

For the past two decades, I have committed to incorporating the teaching of Indigenous and Black authors and texts from both sides of the border regularly in my courses, from a first-year introduction to literature to nation-based courses at the senior levels, often strategically incorporating works that trouble boundaries of various kinds, whether race, sexual orientation, gender, religion, ethnicity, or regional affiliation, to ensure that questions of canonicity are integral to my teaching. Likewise, much of my work as co-editor of *Studies in Canadian Literature/Études en littérature canadienne* has been devoted to foregrounding the study of Indigenous literatures as well as promoting diversity within and beyond the borders of CanLit, a task made much easier by my co-editor's expertise in postcolonial literatures for the decade during which we ran the journal together. In a trial by fire, he had inherited the journal within a year of arriving at UNB, another example of the opportunities and challenges of being part of a smaller department.

Nonetheless, as well-known Black Canadian scholar, author, and activist Rinaldo Walcott reminded CanLit scholars at the May 2017 TransCanadas conference, part of a series of academic conferences intended to raise fundamental questions about CanLit as an institutionalized field of study, claims to inclusivity and radical politics remain empty words when academic positions are "dominated by whiteness." Walcott is right. As the author of what has been described as the "seminal treatise on Black Canadian culture," *Black Like Who?* (1997), Walcott used the conference as opportunity to reflect on CanLit's sustained failure to recognize and "take seriously... Black literary expression" by publicly announcing that he was "quitting CanLit" (Barrett et al.). This kind of scholarly drama is unusual for academic conferences and may seem irrelevant to those beyond CanLit's borders, but Walcott's decision to do so, along with his challenge to the dominant whiteness of CanLit, resonated deeply with me. I may be an ally but I am a settler scholar with my own set of privileges. I cross the Canada-US border with relative impunity because of my skin colour, class, occupation, sexual orientation, and Canadian passport. While I may like to think of myself as an interloper, a betrayer of CanLit loyalties because so much of my scholarship and teaching is so fundamentally premised on an Indigenous refusal to see the Canada-US border as sacrosanct, and someone whose research has never really been strictly Canadian, the fact I got hired two decades ago means someone thought I ticked the boxes enough. And those same boxes remain.

Moreover, I have benefited from the very borders I want so badly to subvert. The current structure of English departments and the majority of job ads within the discipline remains tied to upholding national boundaries, firmly entrenched and frequently monitored national boundaries, though recent ads for transatlantic literary posts make me hopeful that academic borders are becoming more porous. The onus rests on senior scholars like myself to demand and insist on change from within the academy—in other words, to reject the very boxes that secured our careers, even tenuously in my case. Most overtly, at my institution I believe it means fighting for diverse academic appointments across the fields and disciplines, engaging in curricular reform to acknowledge the ways in which nation-states have imposed and continue to enforce imperializing borders, and, most importantly, recognizing the ways in which universities and departments sanction and perpetuate racialized and sexualized hierarchies by virtue of their very structure, even when located geographically and economically on the margins.

Whose CanLit
Solidarity and Accountability in Literary Communities

KRISTEN DARCH AND FAZEELA JIWA

We've been discussing issues of misogyny and racism in CanLit and its institutions for over ten years; an understanding of literature through feminist front-line work is the premise of our friendship. We met while we were both doing anti-violence work through women's shelters and transition houses, and we were both interested in writing as art and feminist praxis. Through our literary political connection, we support each other in the challenging work of deepening our analyses. This meaningful solidarity is what community provides. We excerpt our recent thinking about the concept of community here.

K: The moment of #UBCAccountable did not so much create divisions within "CanLit" as deepen the gendered, classed, raced, and, in some cases, generational divisions that were already there, which are erased in the many media descriptions of CanLit as a "tight-knit community." I want to unpack the term *community*, as it has been used repeatedly in the mainstream media in reference to the landscape of literary production in Canada. What does a community look like—and what doesn't it look like? Who is included and who is not included? If community is understood as a group of people who support each other, have each other's best interests at heart, and believe that what is for the good of one is for the good of the group, is the "CanLit community" really a community?

F: Not based on that definition. Maybe if the word *community* encompasses the uneven power relations that so often go unacknowledged. Canada itself is often described as a "multicultural community" where everyone is "included," but that overlooks the dynamics of who gets to say we are included, who gets to define what we are included into, and what happens when we don't actually want to be included in the kind of community that is on offer. CanLit has had its own fluctuations alongside these official politics. I think it's worth noting that national canons generally create and uphold an uncritical sense of nationalism; the context of Canadian litera-ture—the writing, publishing, and teaching of it—from its inception, was meant to solidify a nationalist project on stolen land. The canon and the mainstream literary community that emerged has been built alongside genocide and ongoing settler colonialism. These industries have always been and still are, on the whole, structurally biased against people outside of the dominant white, male conception of personhood.

There have always been artists and writers who demand accountability from cultural production, though accountability looks different based on the context in which it is demanded. For example, since at least the 1970s, writers, artists, and academics who speak from the margins have been advo-cating for inclusion into a white mainstream of literature, publishing, and academia—Lee Maracle has described how she had to literally storm the stage at a literary festival to be acknowledged, though it was happening on her Nation's land.[1] And the nineties were an incredible time for writers from marginalized groups being included into spaces from which they were pre-viously excluded; events like the Writing Thru Race conference aimed to grow a nascent space for coalition-building between peoples of colour and Indigenous peoples, and classic books by people of colour were published, like *No Language Is Neutral* by Dionne Brand, *Disappearing Moon Cafe* by SKY

Lee, *Cereus Blooms at Night* by Shani Mootoo, *Kiss of the Fur Queen* by Tomson Highway, *The Kappa Child* by Hiromi Goto, *Whylah Falls* by George Elliott Clarke, and so many more!

But it seems that this inclusion, so firmly based in that time's politics of official multiculturalism—itself a nationalist project—also led to co-optation and disappointment, because CanLit didn't meaningfully change. It was not accountable to the people it "included"; despite the fact that a few folks made it in literary institutions as a result of community agitation, in hindsight it seems clear it was not on their own terms. The community may have opened to a select few, but those in power were still white dudes. They still are, mostly.

K: I engage with Canadian literature and the literary community because I think language can heal and reach people, not to enter into a tradition or hierarchy of venerated authors. I don't give a shit about the canon. And that shouldn't be a prerequisite of belonging.

As it is now, CanLit can more accurately be described as a professional network that favours those who are socially constructed to be influential. For it to function as a community that is supportive, there needs to be account-ability to the members who are most vulnerable. If it doesn't quickly and effectively build accountability mechanisms, CanLit stands to lose the voices and the contributions of all those authors who find its institutions hostile, and that means a loss for Canadian readers who find resonance, richness, learning, healing, challenge, understanding, and growth in their words.

What could it look like for members of CanLit institutions who have not suffered from systemic violence to be accountable to members who have, and who occupy a lower place in the hierarchy? How can a famous professor or author or publisher be accountable to people who were con-cerned about their professional conduct—who claim harm as a result of their behaviour—in a way that strengthens community?

Both sides have to be willing for these conversations to unfold in a way that is meaningful.

F: You're probably right, and those are important questions. And there are also so many reasons to protect ourselves by not engaging with folks who refuse to consider other perspectives because they are blinded by their own. It's a risk to put yourself into situations where you are the minority, and we can protect ourselves from ignorance, hurt, and painstaking emotional labour by not doing so. Sometimes, accountability to yourself means that you protect yourself from yet another predictably patterned conversation. But other times, that fact is unsatisfying to me, because in the moment it absolves people with power from having to be accountable—from having to listen, to reckon with the challenge to their structural privilege. Of everyone, they should hear it the most. They can then choose to ignore or belittle others, or they can be open to being thoughtful and maybe even impacted by the generosity of those who take the time to share their experiences.

It's solidarity that's missing in the CanLit "community" when it's defined as simply a grouping of reputable literary people. Solidarity precedes the action that accountability requires; from my perspective, solidarity means that even if you don't have material conditions similar to others in your community, you commit to the hard work of learning the structure of privilege, acknowledging your unearned power, and then giving it up to others who don't have it. That is when accountability happens. Accountability is taking material actions that have the ability to change the material conditions of those who need to be accounted to—those who have less power.

K: Yes. We talk about writers like they are a tight-knit community operating on a level playing field. I have experienced more of a sense of community with my co-workers in the social-housing projects where I worked in Vancouver, because we shared the same material conditions: low income, related low social status, insecure housing causing us to move multiple times a year, often backgrounds of trauma that led us into social work, and often with multiple experiences of marginalization based on race, gender, gender expression, sexuality, and class. These material conditions affect your ability to be a writer and be recognized as such, and they vary so much from writer to writer. The fact is, the "community" that the newspapers refer to is a group of people competing over a limited number of grants and awards and work opportunities, and an even more limited number of well-paid positions.

F: Yes, and if you're materially disadvantaged, then you are vulnerable to people who have those slivers of power, combined with unearned structural privilege. Your reputation is at stake if you don't play the industry's game.

K: The version of community I'd like to build is not about reputation, it is about deeply believing in what the other is trying to do, it is about believing in the importance of the other existing in this world as a writer, believing in the importance of the other continuing to do what she does, continuing to think and react and share her perspective.

F: That's a great definition of community! But the historical and contemporary context of CanLit is a system of neo-liberal capitalism, built on racist patriarchy, which makes a literary career that doesn't capitulate to it extremely difficult. I think that's why artists and writers are increasingly choosing to define success on their own various terms rather than through awards and canons.

K: For myself, if I aim to continue to try to write and publish, I will have to define success differently than belonging to a false notion of community. To me this doesn't look like people with more power validating me, but people with the same amount or less power telling me they feel validated by what I write. When I was younger, street-involved, and could barely imagine graduating high school, I looked to literature for any sign that my perspective was real and to see my truths reflected back to me while my life was on the verge of being lost to violence and addiction. Success, for me, would be making space for those young women now. Our task now is to build new literary communities that are more supportive, more inclusive.

F: And toward that end, I think success no longer means only inclusion—it necessarily means transformation. It's acknowledging that everyone has multiple communities that overlap; we are intersectional beings. Most importantly, it's building up those communities. Right now, I see hundreds of variously marginalized people reaching out to each other to support each other materially, to share information, to write and speak and act to change things. That's success! That's accountability. These everyday, small actions are where radical transformation is most palpable. It is not created from within the structures that are already available. It's slowly built, through cherishing what our elders know and simultaneously celebrating the newest thinking within our intricate communities—that wonderful and difficult process that Lillian Allen describes as "learning to listen to what you don't know you don't know."

K: To me, a transformed CanLit looks like more books published by more people on the peripheries of and outside of circles of power.

F: Yes! In my own work as an editor, my focus is to help folks who have been previously marginalized express their thoughts as accurately and effectively as possible. I work with authors and publishers who are committed to radical social justice. I want cultural production in Canada to be overtaken by the brilliant words, ideas, emotions, and images that writers and artists from non-dominant groups have always created. I want that brilliance to be impossible to ignore. The most optimistic cells in my brain think that's happening right now, even despite the cynical ones that tell me not to get my hopes up, that without vigilance this movement will be co-opted, that institutional change is not forthcoming and power has to be taken. I think it's being taken. Clearly, we're not politely asking for it.

K: I feel the same way. We entered into this dark place as a kind of community starting in November 2016. Hardly anybody got out unscathed. I'd like to say there were no winners; for the first time, CanLit wasn't about winners. It wasn't a shiny gold hallway of repute. It was about complicity, accountability, self-reflection. The world of CanLit, or the spaces of writing and publishing, look and feel different to me than before. Conversations that could barely see the light of day without being shut down, before these events, are now out in the open. In the current climate, I don't feel like I have to fight so hard, because even though we are up against silencing and litigation, now I know there is an audience for whom what I am saying makes sense, because these conversations are finally breaking out into the public, if not in national magazines and papers, then on social media. I now feel more empowered to redirect my energy toward refining my points and what I'm trying to say, even experimenting with form—which is what I should have been doing as a writer all along. Not fighting to prove to various gatekeepers that the issues we're talking about even exist.

Hearing the Artificial Obvious
Margaret Atwood, UBCAccountable, and the Power of Listening

ERIKA THORKELSON

Based upon the article "Margaret Atwood's Books Taught Me to Listen to Women—Now She Needs to Learn the Same Thing," as first published on Electric Literature *(electricliterature.com).*

Writers are often great observers, but we aren't always good listeners. Our stories share knowledge and create empathy in the reader, but the dark side of our work is the ego it sometimes takes to sustain it. Writing, especially something as long and thankless as an entire book, requires a belief in the importance of one's own voice, even in the face of skeptics and critics. We rely on our words to crawl into hearts and change minds. In fact, though, there are times when the most radical thing those with powerful voices can do is listen.

In the wake of Steven Galloway's suspension from the University of British Columbia's Creative Writing Program, where I earned my MFA, the divide between writers who were willing to listen and those who were not became very clear. More precisely, many showed they had drawn a line between who was worth listening to and who was not. Margaret Atwood was one such author.

Before I started university and began to think of myself as a writer, Atwood's books taught me to listen to women's stories in particular, that women's stories were just as important as men's. Her protagonists survived monstrous political oppression in *The Handmaid's Tale*, and a kind of Armageddon in the Maddaddam trilogy. Yet it was my first reading of *Cat's Eye* when I was nineteen years old that taught me that women's stories could be the focus of a narrative unto themselves. Though I'd read many books before this that centred on female characters, their lives had primarily been driven and shaped by their relationships with men. The story of a young girl's journey from a wild childhood in the backwoods of Ontario with her entomologist father to the claustrophobic social hierarchy of a traditional school and into adulthood, *Cat's Eye* was the first book I read that looked at female friendships in a sustained and serious way. Women could be villains to each other. We could be tragic, cruel, smart, and resilient. In other words, we were precisely as complex and fully human as men. None of this seems particularly revolutionary now, but at the time Atwood's work changed the way I viewed myself and the women in my life. It challenged me to take my own story seriously. Yet in the past few years, she has shown that her ability to tell compelling stories about fictional women far outstrips her ability to listen to real ones.

My split with Atwood began in November 2016 with her signing of the UBCAccountable open letter and an editorial she published on *The Walrus* website explaining why. Like many of the other UBCA signatories, her position seemed reasonable on the surface: "the UBC process was flawed and failed both sides." Yet, the few short paragraphs of the editorial focused almost entirely on the ways that accused men would be unfairly treated, ignoring the long, horrible history of women being erased and destroyed in the reporting process. She invoked the "model of the Salem Witchcraft Trials" and the shadow of Steven Truscott, who was wrongfully accused of raping and murdering his classmate Lynne Harper in 1959, when he was just fourteen years old. Atwood also obliquely took on the Believe Women movement that had been seeking to shift the default position of harsh skepticism toward women who accused men of rape or sexual harassment. "To take the position that the members of a group called 'women' are always right and never lie . . . ," she wrote, "would do a great disservice to accusing women and abuse survivors, since it discredits any accusations immediately." If we wanted to know the truth about what was going on at UBC, she argued, the press should contact Joseph Boyden and Madeleine Thien, both of whom I knew to be close friends and vocal supporters of Galloway. Then she used her considerable Twitter presence to bite back at anyone who disagreed with her.

In January 2018, Atwood returned to the topic, this time in the *Globe and Mail*. In an article entitled "Am I a Bad Feminist?" she calls out the women who criticized her for signing the UBCAccountable open letter, positioning herself as a rational being standing for justice against a backlash of orthodox feminist zealots. "It seems that I am a 'Bad Feminist,'" she begins, perhaps accidentally evoking the title of Roxane Gay's book of essays of the same name (Gay later clapped back on Twitter saying, "Actually, Margaret . . . with all due respect, this isn't what I meant by Bad Feminist"). With her trademark acerbic wit, Atwood gives accounts of the many accusations she's endured over the years—being a "dominatrix" or "climbing to fame up a pyramid of decapitated men's heads." She claims that same complexity I found so intoxicating in her stories of women all those years ago, arguing that women "are human beings, with the full range of saintly and demonic behaviours this entails, including criminal ones." Yet, once again, she tells the story from the point of view of Galloway, claiming he had been exonerated "after an inquiry by a judge that went on for months." Throughout, she centres herself as a victim of "Good Feminist accusers" who have already "made up their minds." She ignores the many writers who tried to speak to her personally in the wake of UBCAccountable, the work of Alicia Elliott or then-UBC student Elaine Corden. She ends by calling for unity, which is admirable, but asks that readers unify under her version of the narrative in support of her reputation as a feminist rather than each other. "A war among women, as opposed to a war on women, is always pleasing to those who do not wish women well," she cautions. What she doesn't seem to realize is that criticism of her involvement in UBCAccountable was never about her right to express her opinion. It was about the moral responsibility we all have to choose when to speak and when to listen.

It was disappointing to see this literary hero of my youth return again and again to national publications to argue on behalf of Galloway and UBCAccountable. Before she spoke out, I often defended Atwood against criticism about her prickly public persona. Being a woman writer in Canadian literature, I argued, meant developing a hard shell. The CBC archives are full of evidence of Atwood employing her acidic wit to cut down interviewers who ask silly questions about her domestic life, questions they would never consider asking a man. In one television interview from 1977, when interviewer Hana Gartner suggests that the stories in her collection *Dancing Girls* paint a depressing picture of relationships, Atwood suggests she might prefer reading Harlequin Romance novels.

I remember coming across her poem "You Fit into Me" in a CanLit textbook in undergrad and laughing so hard I cried.

> You fit into me
> like a hook into an eye
> a fish hook
> an open eye

She begins with a cliché line from a love poem and an innocuous metaphor that might come from fashion or sewing and shifts it immediately into something wince-inducing. I love how visceral the image of the fish hook in the open eye is, how in a few lines it demolishes love poetry as a kind of violence. In her public persona and in her writing, she offered a thrilling, confident alternative to the pliant girl that people expected me to be.

Though she comes from a background of far more privilege than I do, Atwood's uncompromising refusal to soften to the expectations of a woman writer was inspiring. From her and those who came slightly before—Alice Munro, Margaret Laurence—I learned that women of my mother's and grandmother's generations lived under a never-ending campaign aimed at breaking down their self-trust. They often worked in isolation and in competition with each other, forced to advocate for themselves against a system that would rather they disappear. Having Atwood's texts gave me a foundation of strength. I thought she would appreciate seeing the same uncompromising commitment to change in the generations that followed her, that she might be willing to use those carefully honed tools to support us. I thought she would be willing to listen to us just as she had forced the world to listen to her.

In the months and years after the allegations against Galloway came to light, I learned repeatedly that listening was not something that Atwood and the other signatories of the UBCAccountable letter were accustomed to. I had conversations online and in person with writers I'd known for years who wanted to do nothing more than attack me or tear down the complainants. It didn't seem to occur to them that others might have more information than they did. As they wrote press releases and personal statements demanding transparency and justice, never once did they think to contact the Main Complainant, through her lawyer or through other complainants who've named themselves in newspaper articles. The signatories said they felt bullied, but it never occurred to them that they might *be* bullies, too, ones with the ability to control the narrative on a much grander scale than their detractors.

Even those writers with good intentions have forgotten to listen at crucial moments. In early 2018, Concordia University graduate Mike Spry purchased a website entitled *CanLit Accountable* to house a single piece of writing—a 4,300-word essay outing himself as complicit in the culture of toxic masculinity that he saw as permeating Concordia's Creative Writing department and Canadian publishing in general. The essay's appearance set off a whole new explosion of conversation in CanLit about the men who hold the power in creative writing programs and how they use that power. Yet nowhere in the entire treatise does Spry mention talking to the women directly affected by the violence he is writing about. Emma Healey's 2014 essay, "Stories Like Passwords," which was a watershed moment for conversations about sexual assault and harassment in CanLit and beyond, is referenced throughout Spry's essay, yet when Healey shared it on Twitter the day it was released, she was as surprised by it as the rest of the world.[1]

But this isn't the only issue that Spry's piece brings up. In her essay "A... Then a Man Said It," writer and Concordia graduate Julie McIsaac points out that these conversations around rape culture and toxic masculinity have been going on amongst women in private for a long time, and that a woman like Healey has far more to lose when she talks about her own experiences. She concludes by pointing out the irony that those in power often ignore these issues when women are the ones doing the talking: "And then a man said it, so now everyone is listening." Without consultation, even well-meaning advocacy can feel a lot like aggression.

It's not that I'm angry with Atwood and those other UBCAccountable signatories. More than anything, I'm sad for them. I see them as people who, out of fear or carelessness, have hardened themselves against the voices of those who have less power and a smaller platform. They have robbed themselves of a great deal of wonder by deafening themselves to certain voices. In her book *Pilgrim at Tinker Creek*, Annie Dillard writes about what happens when we put aside our assumptions about what we deem normal and construct an "artificial obvious" that allows us to see new and extraordinary things (18). Dillard watches the air, the grass, the trees with patience and openness, and the world rewards her with incredible beauty. I believe this principle can be applied to listening, too.

Really listening requires full body presence. It requires you to soften and let go of the fear, the urge to argue, and the instinct to control the narrative. It takes a comfort with silence and a willingness to accept that your turn to talk may never come, that what's happening might not be about you at all. This doesn't mean internalizing every call-out on social media, but rather acknowledging how your voice carries and reaching out to those who have less power with compassion, respect, and openness. It requires you to see them first as individual human beings with names, lives, and experiences you might not have imagined. We've assumed for too long that the onus for reaching out is on the less powerful. We must work to upend that imbalance and make space for women of colour, Indigenous women, trans women, disabled women, and others who have been left out of feminism in the past.

Over the past few years, I've been working on tempering my voice to make more space for listening. I've seen the beauty this openness reveals first-hand in the students I've worked with who come from different linguistic backgrounds and struggle with academic English. A few have told me about teachers who have dismissed them out of hand, assumed they weren't worth listening to, or spoken over them. I've never met a student who didn't have something worth saying inside them. Some just take more time than others.

Indeed, we live in a time when there are endless opportunities to learn about the stories of others in their own words. Not long after CanLitAccountable reignited the conversation around rape culture and publishing came the first anniversary of the Women's March. On a rain-soaked Saturday morning, I stood with a thousand other women and allies on a windy shelf overlooking Vancouver's spectacular North Shore Mountains and heard Musqueam activist Rhiannon Bennett speak about the way the issues addressed by the #MeToo movement disproportionately affect Indigenous women. I heard Hailey Heartless argue with wit and clarity for the life-and-death necessity of including sex workers like herself in feminist discussions. I wiped away tears as Noor Fadel read her poem "I Forgive You," addressed to the man who attacked her on a crowded SkyTrain for wearing a hijab. As woman after woman told stories of violence, familiar and unfamiliar, I felt awed and grateful, even when the things they said called attention to the many privileges I hold as a white cis woman who was born in Canada. Some have condemned this multiplicity of voices as a descent into disorder and chaos. I see it as an opportunity to move toward an equitable society.

The greatest block to really listening is not the noise of the world, but that voice inside that protects us, centres us, rattles with outrage or disbelief. I still respect the ways Atwood made space for women's narratives in literature against tremendous pressure, but I can't help but feel like all those years of protecting herself are what's holding her back from hearing the voices of the women around her now, making it difficult for her to see the beauty in this moment. If we're going to find a way forward, we're all going to have to learn to listen.

· ERIKA THORKELSON

Writing as a Rupture
A Breakup Note to CanLit

JOSHUA WHITEHEAD

In nêhiyawêwin we differentiate language as animate or inanimate rather than masculine and feminine—we acknowledge rocks, trees, rivers, and skies as living things—, as animate, and we are thereby beholden and accountable to them, they are our relations. Within those relations, I too hold my/our stories to that same accountability, we are gifted them through/by the land and we too owe something in return. But whiteness has a knack for animation too, where it extracts hi/story from our bones, which is to say our land but mean our bodies, curates it for museums and archives, skins our stories, empties the land of genealogy and rewrites social progression as a series of vanishing acts. Whiteness loves to re-animate Indigeneity where it sees fit, just ask poor old Wenjack. This country is a graveyard is a haunted house is a necropolis. I sheath myself in Cree and hold my wîhkask to my heart, which really means I hold nohkom cause ain't that her gorgeous hair? I write a break-up note to CanLit but exit the letter saying kîhtwâm, see you again, soon, once more, because we never say goodbye in nêhiyawêwin.

I think of what my colleagues have said to me, "If you finish this degree you'll be the first Indigenous person to complete this program." I will myself do this exhaustive work to etch space for the Indigenous folks I foresee coming after me. I work for the youth, for my niece, cousins, I work for those kids in Attawapiskat, Wapekeka, Pikangikum, I think of my home, Peguis, and the people I've lost there—I think about all the kin who gave their lives in order for me to survive and all of the Elders who gifted me their stories in order for me to thrive. My writing is not fundamentally mine and what I owe is vast, expansive—I am accountable to my communities even if CanLit is not. I think of manitôwâpow of wînipêk, which is to say I work like water: a hard throttle of a wave against a blockage, grinding energy against an aggregate that has mineralized into an obstacle. I shave off a layer through my own type of friction, which is to say my own type of fiction, by which I really mean I sling stories like arrowheads, and watch as this mineraloid dissolves in the wake of my seething. What nipiy tells me is that beneath the foil of a rock bedazzled with sunspots is anything but a core, there is no centre, only coils of askiy, our nikâwiy, only us, the land, mirrored, fractured into infinite shards of quartz. I think of CanLit as that rock full of stagnate breath, canon condensed into a blockage when really it's more a collection of mirrors that have amalgamated into a reflective system spelling out nationalism—a whole thing rather than a web of fractures. The water teaches me that these systems come apart, that nothing is whole; rock is porous as are stories, both of which come from the land and return to it.

Setting is a, if not *the*, character here on Turtle Island and these character(s) in y/our literatures have always been Indigenous.

To me, storytelling is a synonym for accountability.

Literature is always kissing a certain type of kinship.

Recently I watched *Spider-Man: Homecoming* and something caught my attention in the film's opening scene: it features Michael Keaton as an antagonist, The Vulture, having a conversation with Michael Chernus. They are holding a portrait of The Avengers drawn by a youth. "Things are never going to be the same now," narrates Keaton, "I mean, look at this, you got aliens, you got big green guys tearing down buildings. When I was a kid I used to draw cowboys and Indians." He is quickly corrected by Chernus, "Actually, it's Native Americans." Keaton's character takes a brief reprieve,

"Tell you what though, it ain't bad, is it?" Chernus' character agrees, "No, yeah, kid's got a future" much to the dismay of Keaton, "Yeah, well, we'll see I guess." I was drawn to this scene for its attempt at playfulness regarding Indigeneity, adolescence, and futurisms. The scene pans to the crumbling Avengers Tower. We then witness Keaton's team excavating an alien structure that looks akin to a fossilized carcass, something that pre/post-dates their arrival by some time, something Indigenous to its own land base and to its own world, a fossilized cadaver they dissect in order to manufacture militarized bioweapons and nanotechnologies. This scene rings too true to the current state of Indigeneity on Turtle Island, our literatures, and the buffering of an amalgamated Canadian canon.[1]

Maybe that's why I think that literature is an augmentation, is the decadence of anthropology, the end result(s) of excavation and its institutional grants, it's the glamorized tale(s) of fossil fuels and land/bodies. I think of my nêhiyaw cousin who watches these films religiously, dresses up like these superheroes and aspires to be them through play. I think of Chris Hemsworth, the actor of Thor, who appropriated Indigeneity in order to "play Indian" during a Lone Ranger themed party. I wonder what kind of mirrors are being crafted and for who? What is it that people think Indigeneity looks like? What is interpolated for them psychically and physically when they swish that word around in their mouths, when those syllables spring from their tongues?" I think, that's *paleo*ntology—albeit it by cannibalizing the Huron or calling for a prize in the best showmanship of appropriation.

Another boulder in the waterway.

I take a cue from my Two-Spirit cybernetic trickster, zoa, and learn to re-augment my body: transgressive, punk, Indigiqueer. I place myself into the film, Oji-Cree in NYC, and look up at that crumbling tower in glee. I watch the structure come apart at its seams, laugh, think, "Yeah, that kid does have a future that you will see." Tell those vultures, by which I mean wendigo, that they're colour blind—that big green guy tearing down buildings is the mihko mistahâpêw, Red Hulk, tearing down structures and institutions. If Indigeneity is a vanishing act it's one we've perfected to ghost ourselves into the future, just ask Frenchie, Jared Martin, and all those Two-Spirit hero(ines) who learned to live and love beyond body, space, and time. Here I am attaching those loosened minerals to my skin to emerge a diamond crusted NDN, full-metal and vicious in the light. I am not a whole thing; I am a web of fractures living in my brokenness—web like okimâw apihkêsîs, trickster spider, who spun the original world-wide-web, all sticky with feeling and smooth as a weathered pebble.

Connection is a technology Indigeneity perfected.

I write to world-build, to define resurgence in and through my body. I think of my degrees and writing tutelage I underwent. During the beginning of my BA I entered Creative Writing, there I was told to mimic the greats: Fitzgerald, Whitman, Eliot, Laurence, Atwood, Martel. I learned to write white and ingrained the mode of thinking that art is apolitical, that a good story is a reflection of the times but that those times never strayed too far from settler exceptionalism. I wonder how well of a writer each would be if there weren't at least a semblance of appropriation in their writing? I recall being told not to write of genre and to avoid too many "issues" as it cluttered the page. I can't help but think that those professors were saying: your body clutters our institutions. My body is an oration is a braille narrative is a petroglyph; to extract it from how I navigate the world/page is to ask me to annihilate myself.

: ::: :::::: ::: :: ::: :: ::: ::::: :::: ::: :::: : :: : :::: :: ::: :: ::: ::: ::: ::: :: : : :: :: ::: ::: :::: ::::: ::: : : : :::: :
:::: : :::::: : :::: : ::: : :: ::: ::: ::::: :: : :::: :: : ::: :: : :: :::: :: ::: :: : :: : : :: :: : :::: :: : : ::: : : :::
: ::: :::::: ::: :: ::: :: ::: ::::: :::: ::: :::: : :: : :::: :: ::: :: ::: ::: ::: ::: :: : : :: :: ::: ::: :::: ::::: ::: : : : :::: :
:::: : :::::: : :::: : ::: : :: ::: ::: ::::: :: : :::: :: : ::: :: : :: :::: :: ::: :: : :: : : :: :: : :::: :: : : ::: : : :::
: ::: :::::: ::: :: ::: :: ::: ::::: :::: ::: :::: : :: : :::: :: ::: :: ::: ::: ::: ::: :: : : :: :: ::: ::: :::: ::::: ::: : : : :::: :
:::: : :::::: : :::: : ::: : :: ::: ::: ::::: :: : :::: :: : ::: :: : :: :::: :: ::: :: : :: : : :: :: : :::: :: : : ::: : : :::
: ::: :::::: ::: :: ::: :: ::: ::::: :::: ::: :::: : :: : :::: :: ::: :: ::: ::: ::: ::: :: : : :: :: ::: ::: :::: ::::: ::: : : : :::: :
:::: : :::::: : :::: : ::: : :: ::: ::: ::::: :: : :::: :: : ::: :: : :: :::: :: ::: :: : :: : : :: :: : :::: :: : : ::: : : :::
: ::: :::::: ::: :: ::: :: ::: ::::: :::: ::: :::: : :: : :::: :: ::: :: ::: ::: ::: ::: :: : : :: :: ::: ::: :::: ::::: ::: : : : :::: :
:::: : :::::: : :::: : ::: : :: ::: ::: ::::: :: : :::: :: : ::: :: : :: :::: :: ::: :: : :: : : :: :: : :::: :: : : ::: : : :::
: ::: :::::: ::: :: ::: :: ::: ::::: :::: ::: :::: : :: : :::: :: ::: :: ::: ::: ::: ::: :: : : :: :: ::: ::: :::: ::::: ::: : : : :::: :
:::: : :::::: : :::: : ::: : :: ::: ::: ::::: :: : :::: :: : ::: :: : :: :::: :: ::: :: : :: : : :: :: : :::: :: : : ::: : : :::
: ::: :::::: ::: :: ::: :: ::: ::::: :::: ::: :::: : :: : :::: :: ::: :: ::: ::: ::: ::: :: : : :: :: ::: ::: :::: ::::: ::: : : : :::: :
:::: : :::::: : :::: : ::: : :: ::: ::: ::::: :: : :::: :: : ::: :: : :: :::: :: ::: :: : :: : : :: :: : :::: :: : : ::: : : :::

::: :: :If living is a political act, let me extend, fill the body of this narration with *my* body: :: :: :
:: Witness me in my fragmented fashion, let me hack what an essay is supposed to look like::
:::: : :::::: : :::: : ::: : :: ::: ::: ::::: :: : :::: :: : ::: :: : :: :::: :: ::: :: : :: : : :: :: : :::: :: : : ::: : : :::
: ::: :::::: ::: :: ::: :: ::: ::::: :::: ::: :::: : :: : :::: :: ::: :: ::: ::: ::: ::: :: : : :: :: ::: ::: :::: ::::: ::: : : : :::: :
:::: : :::::: : :::: : ::: : :: ::: ::: ::::: :: : :::: :: : ::: :: : :: :::: :: ::: :: : :: : : :: :: : :::: :: : : ::: : : :::
: ::: :::::: ::: :: ::: :: ::: ::::: :::: ::: :::: : :: : :::: :: ::: :: ::: ::: ::: ::: :: : : :: :: ::: ::: :::: ::::: ::: : : : :::: :
:::: : :::::: : :::: : ::: : :: ::: ::: ::::: :: : :::: :: : ::: :: : :: :::: :: ::: :: : :: : : :: :: : :::: :: : : ::: : : :::
: ::: :::::: ::: :: ::: :: ::: ::::: :::: ::: :::: : :: : :::: :: ::: :: ::: ::: ::: ::: :: : : :: :: ::: ::: :::: ::::: ::: : : : :::: :
:::: : :::::: : :::: : ::: : :: ::: ::: ::: :: :: ::: :: : : be like: : :: :::: :: : :: :: ::: :: ::: ::: ::::: : :: ::: ::: ::: : : :
: ::: :::::: ::: :: ::: :: ::: ::::: :::: ::: :::: : :: : :::: :: ::: :: ::: ::: ::: ::: :: : : :: :: ::: ::: :::: ::::: ::: : : : :::: :
:::: : :::::: : :::: : ::: : :: ::: ::: ::::: :: : :::: :: : ::: :: : :: :::: :: ::: :: : :: : : :: :: : :::: :: : : ::: : : :::
: ::: :::::: ::: :: ::: :: ::: ::::: :::: ::: :::: : :: : :::: :: ::: :: ::: ::: ::: ::: :: : : :: :: ::: ::: :::: ::::: ::: : : : :::: :
:::: : :::::: : :::: : ::: : :: ::: ::: :::: :: :::: :: : me&break ::: :: : :: :::: :: : :: :: ::: :: ::: ::: ::::: :: : : :: : : :::
: ::: :::::: ::: :: ::: :: ::: ::::: :::: ::: :::: : :: : :::: :: ::: :: ::: ::: ::: ::: :: : : :: :: ::: ::: :::: ::::: ::: : : : :::: :
:::: : :::::: : :::: : ::: : :: ::: ::: ::::: :: : :::: :: : ::: :: : :: :::: :: ::: :: : :: : : :: :: : :::: :: : : ::: : : :::
: ::: :::::: ::: :: :: :: ::: :::: their::: ::: :::: : :: : : :::: :: :: ::: ::: :: ::: ::: ::: :: ::: :: :: :: :::: ::: : : :
:::: : :::::: : :::: : ::: : :: ::: ::: ::::: :: : :::: :: : ::: :: : :: :::: :: ::: :: : :: : : :: :: : :::: :: : : ::: : : :::
: ::: :::::: ::: :: ::: :: ::: ::::: :::: ::: :::: : :: : :::: :: ::: :: ::: ::: ::: ::: :: : : :: :: ::: ::: :::: ::::: ::: : : : :::: :
:::: : :::::: : :::: : ::: : :: ::: ::: ::::: :: : :::: :: : ::: :: : :: :::: :: ::: :: : :: : : :: :: : :::: :: : : ::: :: :: :
:: :::::: ::: :::: : :: : ::: :: ::: :: :: ::: :: : : :: : : :: :: ::: ::: ::::: :: : ::: :: : :: ::: :: ::: ::: :
: ::: :::::: ::: :: ::: :: ::: ::: :::: :::: ::: :: : : :: :: ::: :: :: :: ::: ::: ::: :: : : : :: :: :: ::: :::::: things ::: : :

And when I did write about Indigeneity, my queerness, my gender identity, and/or my culture I was told to either amplify or sequester it. Show, don't tell, that old adage, and writing is a suffering. I can't help but think of how voyeuristic these practices are, like taking a camera into a sweat lodge, there are boundaries that my body has maintained and I respect them even if you think art has no extremities. I think of the writing we're doing now in Indigenous literatures, of imagining futurities, of seeing ourselves t/here, of writing ourselves into different worlds, fourth dimensions, finding kin in space and refuge in horrifying ourselves to terrify. What does it mean to be told to write realism when our livelihoods are those realities?[2] What kind of worlds and refuges do you shut down in turning those modes of thinking off? Can I live as a writer if the life of writing is thought through structures of suffering? I wonder what kind of death-sentence that mode of creation becomes for those who can't fall back into whiteness? If I horrify you, I am sorry, I spell horror a little differently.[3]

Set the stakes, maintain the tension, expand your dynamics, are other writing mantras that have been directed to me. What my teachers meant when demanding that from me was to hyperbolize suffering, to blood-let traumas and splash generations across the page, spell out nonsensical syllabics in order to move my audience and interpolate Indigeneity. I wonder if they think blood memories require blood quantums? Why must I always victimize my characters? What does it look like to write Indigeneity as a normalcy? If I did, would I still be considered an emerging writer from your unions or would my triumphs exceed your expectations of what and how Indigeneity should function and feel? Why can't I be an Indigenous writer who writes of his queerness and femmeness without your mental mappings collapsing? Am I an Indigenous writer if I write a narrative about a non-Indigenous person? Am I still Indigenous if I write about my queerness unabashedly? Am I still Indigenous if I am not stoic, tragic, pained, or dead? I don't like this game so I reiterate: write sounds too close to white, instead say masinahikê and really mean nêhiyawak mahihkanak. I remove myself from your encapsulations. I am not a poet, a novelist, a spoken word artist, nor a performance artist, I am an otâcimow who howls âcimowinisa but follows the tradition of his ancestors; my stories are orations that are printed on the page so I may shower them tectonically. Because of that, I am not CanLit, I am Indigenous Lit, and I follow in the footsteps of those who have paved the way with the weighted press of their omaskisiniwâwa

Why must we always exist within one world if I live within many horizontally and offer tobacco to those I honour vertically? Indigenous Lit will survive without CanLit, we have already, but I am not sure if CanLit can do the same. I humble myself, because that is a sacred teaching, and I look to the future, which really means I avoid lip service and look to the now and think about how we can move together, individually, hand-in-hand. I recall my experience this past year with the New Constellations Tour and sharing the stage with Leanne Betasamosake Simpson, Peter Dreimanis, Leah Fay, Jeremy Dutcher, Elisapie, Damian Rogers, Mob Bounce, Cris Derksen, and Jason Collett. We took to Treaty 7 and we collectively sang our songs, met ourselves through story. I think that's what reconciliation looks like, that collectiveness through individualism, one that sways a pendulum both ways and intersects time like a bow, which is really to say a figure-eight, a Métis optic, an infinity symbol, a post-contact communion. That collaboration that intercepts the isolation of being a writer, the harmonizing of voices into a symphony that maintains the rhythm even when you're out of breath and your diaphragm is resting, voice like a pack howl that startles and staggers, that pines between borders of genre and rattles the canon, shaves off another layer of rock. To remove the written word from the bookshelf and give it back to orality is a powerful decolonial act. Sometimes I wonder if CanLit can be that? Focused less on the craft and more on the gift, less of the page and more of the story, less of the individual and more of the communal? I wonder if CanLit will ever recognize it is part of the ecosystem of this literary nation-state and it too maintains a responsibility and accountability to its land base and those who protect it? Maybe I'll come back to you, CanLit, if you can tell me who you're accountable to, but until then, I ain't got time to heal you too—I have Turtle Island to look forward to.

So I turn to nipiy, dip story into it, watch it emerge refreshed and renewed. Story is a holistic thing, I am not the sole author of what I say, I sit

...ite, stand and orate, as the avatar of all of those who preceded me. Perhaps that's the difference between you and I, CanLit, you write for decorum, recognition, you write for As and medals and compensation while I write simply to survive. I write to nourish, I write to give back because I have communities that nurtured me and now I too am called to nurture back. I write to craft mirrors for my kin to see themselves in, "Here I am, sharp like asiniy, ample as maskihkiy." I am manitôwâpow, the land of water, strait that isn't straight. I've learned to meander when I need to and eddy when I can. If you think of writing as a vacuum then you've swilled us around for too long, here we swell and explode, well to the surface, flood between your hands, feed the land beneath your feet. My writing is a valiant orgasm, all sticky and new in its cytoplasm, I the protoplasm, nuclei dancing into livelihood. When I speak of nipiy I speak of Sky Woman and when I narrate her I sing myself into the world, I'm like the NDN Aphrodite, all sexy and rapturous, emerging from the foam. I think of myself as a rock breaker, and one who gets them off; in this current milieu of an emerging wave of Indigenous literatures I think of my role as the one who grinds—grinds boulders into a medicine washing up after the crest. I hold this nation, and its literatures, finally accountable to me for once, the I who is living, thriving, surviving, the I who animates his selves: nêhiyaw iskwêwiw-nâpêw.

Contributor Bios

JENNIFER ANDREWS teaches in the Department of English at the University of New Brunswick. She has published two books and numerous book chapters and articles about English-Canadian and American literature and Indigenous North American literatures and cultures. She was co-editor of *Studies in Canadian Literature/Études en littérature canadienne* for a decade, has served as Department Chair, and is the current President of the Association of Canadian College and University Teachers of English.

GWEN BENAWAY is of Anishinaabe and Métis descent. She has published two collections of poetry, *Ceremonies for the Dead* and *Passage*. A Two-Spirited Trans poet, she has been described as the spiritual love child of Tomson Highway and Anne Sexton. She has received many distinctions and awards, including the Dayne Ogilvie Honour of Distinction for Emerging Queer Authors from the Writers' Trust of Canada. Her poetry and essays have been published in national publications and anthologies, including the *Globe and Mail*, *Maclean's*, CBC Arts, and many others. She was born in Wingham, Ontario, and currently resides in Toronto.

NATALEE CAPLE is the author of nine books of poetry and fiction. Her work has been nominated for the KM Hunter award, the RBC Bronwyn Wallace Award, the Gerald Lampert Memorial Award, the ReLit Award, and The

Walter Scott Prize for Historical Fiction. Her latest novel, *In Calamity's Wake* was published in Canada by HarperCollins and in the US by Bloomsbury. The novel in translation was published by Boréal and has been sold separately in France. Her new book of poetry, *Love in the Chthulucene/Cthulhucene* will be published by Wolsak and Wynn in Spring 2019. Natalee is an associate professor at Brock University.

MARIE CARRIÈRE directs the Canadian Literature Centre at the University of Alberta, where she is also Professor of English and French. She has published several books, articles, and collections on Canadian, Indigenous, and Québécoises women writers and feminism. She is currently at work on a new book titled *Cautiously Hopeful: Metafeminist Practices in Canada*.

KRISTEN DARCH is a writer of creative non-fiction, editor, and visual artist most recently working in heritage architectural restoration. She holds a BFA in Visual Art and an MFA in Creative Writing.

ALICIA ELLIOTT is a Tuscarora writer from Six Nations of the Grand River living in Brantford, Ontario, with her husband and child. Her essay "A Mind Spread Out on the Ground" won Gold at the National Magazine Awards in 2017. Her short story "Unearth" was selected for *Best American Short Stories 2018*. She was the 2017–18 Geoffrey and Margaret Andrew Fellow at UBC, and was selected by Tanya Talaga as the recipient of the 2018 RBC Taylor Prize Emerging Writer Award. Her book of essays, *A Mind Spread Out on the Ground*, is forthcoming from Doubleday Canada in spring 2019.

KIM GOLDBERG is the author of seven books of poetry and non-fiction. She is a winner of the Rannu Fund Poetry Prize for Speculative Literature, the Goodwin's Award for Excellence in Alternative Journalism, and other distinctions. Her first poetry collection, *Ride Backwards on Dragon* (Leaf Press, 2007), was shortlisted for the Gerald Lampert Memorial Award. Her second collection, *Red Zone* (Pig Squash Press, 2009), about urban homelessness, has been taught in university literature courses. In 2016 she released *Undetectable* (Pig

Squash Press), her haibun journey through a lifetime of hepatitis C and virus as metaphor for colonialism and eco-destruction. Kim lives Nanaimo, BC. Website: pigsquash.wordpress.com/ Twitter: @KimPigSquash

JANE EATON HAMILTON is the author of nine books of creative non-fiction, fiction, and poetry, including the 2016 novel *Weekend* and two prior collections of short fiction. The *Vancouver Sun* called *Weekend* a "tour de force." Hamilton's books have been shortlisted for the Mind Book of the Year Award, the BC Book Prize, the VanCity Award, the Pat Lowther Memorial Award, the Ferro-Grumley Award, and the ReLit Award. Their memoir was one of the UK *Guardian*'s Best Books of the Year and a *Sunday Times* bestseller. They are the two-time winner of Canada's CBC Literary Award for Fiction (2003/2014).

FAZEELA JIWA is an acquisitions and development editor with Fernwood Publishing by day (okay, sometimes by night, too) and a writer of poetry, essays, and creative non-fiction. Reach her at fazeelajiwa.com or @ fazeelajiwa.

SONNET L'ABBÉ, PhD, is the author of *A Strange Relief* and *Killarnoe*, and was the 2014 guest editor of *Best Canadian Poetry in English*. Her chapbook, *Anima Canadensis*, was published by Junction Books in 2016 and won the 2017 bpNichol Chapbook Award. In her next collection, *Sonnet's Shakespeare*, L'Abbé writes over all 154 of Shakespeare's sonnets. L'Abbé is a professor of Creative Writing and English at Vancouver Island University.

DR. LUCIA LORENZI is a SSHRC Postdoctoral Fellow in the Department of English and Cultural Studies at McMaster University. Her research focuses on representations of sexual violence in literature and other media, with a focus on the aesthetic and political uses of silence, as well as perpetrator narratives. She is also trained as a Canadianist, with an emphasis on contemporary novels and drama, as well as Black Canadian literatures. Her work has been published in *Canadian Literature*, *TOPIA: Canadian Journal of Cultural Studies*, and *West Coast Line*.

TANIS MacDONALD's memoir in essays, *Out of Line: Daring to be an Artist Outside the Big City*, was published by Wolsak and Wynn in spring 2018. She is a co-editor (with Ariel Gordon and Rosanna Deerchild) of *GUSH: menstrual manifestos for our times* (Frontenac House, 2018), and was a finalist for the Gabrielle Roy Prize for *The Daughter's Way* (WLUP, 2012). Her creative non-fiction and poetry have appeared in *Prairie Fire, Studies in Canadian Literature, Tessera, New Quarterly*, and *Lemon Hound*, and she is the author of three books of poetry, with the next forthcoming with Book*hug in 2019. Tanis is Associate Professor in the Department of English and Film Studies at Wilfrid Laurier University in Waterloo, Ontario.

Since 1989, novelist and poet **KEITH MAILLARD** has taught in the Creative Writing Program at the University of British Columbia, where he is a full professor. His novels have won or been nominated for a number of awards: *Light in the Company of Women* was a runner-up for the Ethel Wilson Fiction Prize; *Motet* won that prize; *Hazard Zones* was shortlisted for the Commonwealth Literary Prize, *Gloria* shortlisted for the Governor General's Award, and *The Clarinet Polka* was awarded the Creative Arts Prize by the Polish American Historical Association. His poetry collection, *Dementia Americana*, won the 1995 Gerald Lampert Memorial Award for the best first book of poetry published in Canada. He has been honoured by the West Virginia Library Association and by his hometown of Wheeling, West Virginia, where he was inducted into the Hall of Fame. His fourteenth novel, *Twin Studies*, was published by Freehand Books in September 2018. Anyone interested in a fuller account of his life and work might visit his website: keithmaillard.com.

HANNAH McGREGOR is an Assistant Professor of Publishing at Simon Fraser University, a feminist podcaster, and a CanLit killjoy. She co-hosts the popular Harry Potter podcast *Witch, Please*, and hosts the slightly less popular podcast *Secret Feminist Agenda*, a weekly discussion of the insidious, nefarious, insurgent, and mundane ways we enact our feminism in our daily lives. She lives in Vancouver on the territory of the Musqueam, Squamish, and Tsleil-Waututh, and has two cats; one is named after a poet, and the other is named after a breakfast.

LAURA MOSS, PhD, teaches Canadian and African literatures at the University of British Columbia, on the traditional, ancestral, and unceded territory of the Musqueam people. She currently serves as the editor of *Canadian Literature: A Quarterly of Criticism and Review*. In addition to editing *Is Canada Postcolonial?: Unsettling Canadian Literature* and co-editing (with Cynthia Sugars) the two-volume *Canadian Literature in English: Texts and Contexts*, she has published articles on works by Chinua Achebe, Emma Donoghue, Antje Krog, Vincent Lam, Rohinton Mistry, Salman Rushdie, Annabel Soutar, Zadie Smith, M. G. Vassanji, and Rita Wong, among others, and has written on literary pedagogy, public arts policy in Canada, the history of multiculturalism, genetic modification and seed practices, and public art memorials. Three core questions inform her work: Who Speaks for Whom? Who Listens? Who Profits?

DOROTHY ELLEN PALMER is a disabled senior writer, mom, binge knitter, accessibility consultant, retired high school drama/English teacher, and union activist. She is the author of *When Fenelon Falls* (Coach House, 2010), the only book she has ever seen in CanLit about a disabled adoptee. Her memoir, *This Redhead and Her Walker Walk into a Bar*, will be published by Wolsak and Wynn in 2019.

JULIE RAK is a Professor at the University of Alberta who lives and works on Treaty 6 and Métis territory. Julie was a Killam Professor for 2017–18 at her university. She is the author of two books, eight edited collections, and other publications in the areas of life writing and other non-fiction, Canadian literature in English, and book history. With Keavy Martin, she edited the new and way better edition of the landmark memoir about Inuit life, *Life Among the Qallunaat*, with the full participation of author Mini Aodla Freeman. Julie is completing a SSHRC-funded book manuscript, *Social Climbing: Gender in Mountaineering Expedition Writing*, for McGill-Queens University Press, and she promises her editor that she really is almost finished.

A. H. REAUME is a disabled writer and long-time feminist activist with a master's degree in Canadian Literature from UBC. Her writing has been published in the *Globe and Mail*, the *Vancouver Sun*, and many other outlets, and she has won awards for her activist work, which was also mentioned in the textbook *Canadian Women: A History*. She is currently finishing a novel.

NIKKI REIMER is a carbon-based life form residing on the traditional territories of the Treaty 7 people of Southern Alberta (Calgary). She has published two books of poetry: *DOWNVERSE* (Talonbooks) and *[sic]* (Frontenac House), a finalist for the Gerald Lampert Memorial Award. A third collection is forthcoming in 2019. Her work has also been shortlisted for the Lit POP Award and the PRISM International Creative Non-Fiction contest. Creative and non-fiction work has appeared on stages, billboards, public art exhibits, pop-up bistro menus, and in various journals and anthologies. Reimer was a member of the Kootenay School of Writing Collective in Vancouver between the years 2004 to 2006 and 2008 to 2010.

KAI CHENG THOM is a writer, spoken word artist, therapist, and wicked witch. The descendant of Chinese migrant workers on the Canadian Pacific Railway, she is based in Toronto, unceded Indigenous territory. Her writing has been published widely in print and online in *Buzzfeed*, *them*, *Asian American Literary Review*, *Everyday Feminism*, and others. The winner of the 2017 Dayne Ogilvie Prize for LGBT Writers, Kai Cheng is the author of the novel *Fierce Femmes and Notorious Liars*, the poetry collection *a place called No Homeland*, and the children's book *From the Stars in the Sky to the Fish in the Sea*.

ERIKA THORKELSON is a freelance journalist and writer of fiction and creative non-fiction. Her work has appeared in local and national publications, including the *Vancouver Sun*, *Maisonneuve*, *The Walrus*, *Hazlitt*, and *Room* magazine. She's an occasional host of *The Storytelling Show* on Vancouver Co-op Radio and teaches humanities at Emily Carr University of Art + Design.

DR. ZOE TODD (Métis/otipemisiw) is from amiskwaciwâskahikan (Edmonton), Alberta, Canada. She writes about prairie fish, art, Métis legal traditions, the Anthropocene, extinction, and decolonization in urban and prairie contexts. She also studies human-animal relations, colonialism, and environmental change in north/western Canada.

CHELSEA VOWEL is Métis from manitow-sâkahikan (Lac Ste. Anne), Alberta, currently residing in amiskwacîwâskahikan (Edmonton). Mother to six girls, she has a BEd and LLB, and is currently a graduate student and online Cree language coordinator at the Faculty of Native studies at the University of Alberta. Chelsea is a public intellectual, writer, and educator whose work intersects language, gender, Métis self-determination, and resurgence. Co-host of the Indigenous feminist sci-fi podcast *Métis in Space* and author of *Indigenous Writes: A Guide to First Nations, Métis & Inuit Issues in Canada*, Chelsea blogs at apihtawikosisan.com and makes legendary bannock.

PHOEBE WANG's debut collection of poetry, *Admission Requirements*, was nominated for the Trillium Book Award and shortlisted for the 2018 Gerald Lampert Memorial Award and the Pat Lowther Memorial Award. She works as an ELL Writing and Learning Consultant with OCADU and also currently works with Poetry in Voice. She is a first-generation Chinese Canadian and lives in Toronto.

JOSHUA WHITEHEAD is an Ojibway-Cree/nehiyaw, Two-Spirit/Indigiqueer from Peguis First Nation (Treaty 1). He is an otâcimow and scholar completing a PhD in English Literatures with a focus on Indigenous Literatures and Cultures at the University of Calgary on Traditional Blackfoot Territory (Treaty 7). He is the author of *full-metal indigiqueer* and *Jonny Appleseed*.

ERIN WUNKER researches, teaches, and writes in Halifax, Nova Scotia.

LORRAINE YORK is Distinguished University Professor and Senator William McMaster Chair in Canadian Literature and Culture in the Department of

English and Cultural Studies at McMaster University. She is the author of *Literary Celebrity in Canada* (University of Toronto Press, 2007), *Margaret Atwood and the Labour of Literary Celebrity* (University of Toronto Press, 2013), and *Celebrity Cultures in Canada*, co-edited with Katja Lee (Wilfrid Laurier University Press, 2016). Her most recent book, *Reluctant Celebrity*, which examines public displays of celebrity reluctance as forms of privilege intertwined with race, gender, and sexuality, appeared with Palgrave Macmillan in 2018.

Acknowledgements

This book is made possible by the extensive activism and writing of many people, both contributors and those whose work expands beyond this collection: Jen Sookfong Lee, Dina Del Bucchia, Chelsea Rooney, Emma Healey, Amanda Leduc, Karina Vernon, Sachiko Murakami, Daniel Heath Justice, Jesse Wente, Ryan McMahon, Marilyn Dumont, Amy De'ath, Elaine Corden, Roewan Crowe, Camilla Gibb, Erica Violet Lee, Linda Morra, Andrew Bennett, Zoe Whittall, Tracey Lindberg, Canisia Lubrin, Marcelle Kosman, Rebecca Salazar, Vivek Shraya, Adam Pottle, Casey Plett, Amber Dawn, Lindsay Nixon, Natalie Wee, Ivan Coyote, Larissa Lai, Erín Moure, Shannon Maguire, Rob Budde, Bronwyn Wallace, Mandi Grey, Katja Thieme, Leigh Gilmore, Glynnis Stephenson, Peggy McCann, Lily Cho, Samantha Marie Nock, Amanda Spallacci, Meghan Bell, Lorri Neilsen Glenn, Susan Musgrave, Susan Glickman, Beth Driscoll, Millicent Weber, Noelle Allen, Brittany Hubley, Marcus Miller, Shama Rangwala, Carrianne Leung, Jael Richardson, Phinder Dulai, Kevin Macpherson Ekhoff, Sina Queyras, Barbara Godard, Julie Mannell, Leigh Nash, Shazia Hafiz Ramji, Michael Blouin, Sierra Skye Gemma, Gillian Jerome and many, many more, including those whose names we'll never know.

Thanks to everyone who signed the Counter-Letter against UBCAccountable.

Sincere thanks, *kinanaskomitin*, to Dorothy Thunder for her time and expertise.

Kim Golberg's poem "small birds" first appeared in *Event*, Spring 2018, and appears here by permission. Zoe Todd's essay "Rape Culture, CanLit, and You" and Lucia Lorenzi's essay "#CanLit at the Crossroads" appear here by permission of the authors. Alicia Elliott's essay "CanLit Is a Raging Dumpster Fire" first appeared on the *Open Book* site September 2017 and appears here by permission.

Julie thanks Danielle for her love, wisdom, and strength, and Mr. T and Loki for adding feline value to all things. She thanks her co-editors Erin and Hannah, Hazel and Jay at Book*hug, her colleagues and friends who care about these issues and want CanLit to be better than it is, the amazing activists she has met since November 2016, and her students for reminding her every day why she does this work.

Hannah is grateful to her scattered networks, homes, and beloveds in Edmonton and Toronto and Guelph and Ottawa and Halifax and beyond, and to her new community in Vancouver, who have welcomed her into this strange, beautiful, terrible city. She is grateful to Julie for keeping her fierce and Erin for keeping her earnest, to Hazel and Jay for keeping this project realistic and largely on schedule, and to cats for being small and soft and good.

Erin sends love and gratitude to the contributors and the would-be contributors who couldn't but would have had things been different. Like Hannah and Julie, she is grateful to her networks and loved ones near and far, and while she's at it she's thankful for Hannah and Julie, who are full of verve and fire and care so very much. Gratitude to Jay and Hazel. Love to Lucia and Catherine and Fazeela for always texting back. Boundless love to B & E for being my heart's home.

Works Cited

Stars Upon Thars

Bachmann, Brit. "It's Only Castles Burning." *Discorder*. 5 Dec 2016. www.citr.ca/discorder/
dec-2016-jan-2017/its-only-castles-burning/

Bethune, Brian. "How the Steven Galloway Affair Became a CanLit Class War." *Maclean's*. 23 Nov
2016. www.macleans.ca/culture/books/how-the-steven-galloway-affair-became-a-canlit-class-war/

Darbyshire, Peter. "CanLit Stars Pen Open Letter Blasting UBC over the Steven Galloway Affair."
Vancouver Sun. 15 Nov 2016. vancouversun.com/news/local-news/
canlit-stars-pen-open-letter-blasting-ubc-over-the-steven-galloway-affair

Fussell, Paul. *Class: A Guide through the American Status System*. New York: Summit, 1983.

hooks, bell. *where we stand: class matters*. London: Routledge, 2000.

Lederman, Marsha. "Steven Galloway Scandal Creates Divisions in the CanLit World." *Globe and
Mail*. 18 Nov 2016. www.theglobeandmail.com/arts/books-and-media/steven-galloway-scandal-
creates-divisions-in-the-canlit-world/article32928994/

——. "Under a Cloud: How UBC's Steven Galloway Affair Has Haunted a Campus and Changed
Lives." *Globe and Mail*. 28 Oct 2016. www.theglobeandmail.com/news/british-columbia/
ubc-and-the-steven-galloway-affair/article32562653/

Le Guin, Ursula K. "Ursula K. Le Guin's Speech at the National Book Awards: 'Books Aren't Just
Commodities." *Guardian*. 20 Nov 2014. www.theguardian.com/books/2014/nov/20/
ursula-k-le-guin-national-book-awards-speech

Lewis, C. S. *The Screwtape Letters: Letters from a Senior to a Junior Devil*. London: Geoffery Bles, 1942.

Lewsen, Simon. "The CanLit Firestorm." *TheWalrus.ca*. 24 Nov 2016. thewalrus.ca/
the-canlit-firestorm/

Marche, Stephen. (StephenMarche) "An interesting point . . ." 24 Nov 2016. 11:56 a.m. Tweet.

Seuss, Dr. (Theodor Seuss Geisel). *The Sneetches and Other Stories*. New York: Random House, 1961.

Smith, Russell. "Canadian Poetry's Unlikely Renaissance." *Globe and Mail*. 19 Sept 2012. www.
theglobeandmail.com/arts/books-and-media/canadian-poetrys-unlikely-renaissance/
article4554863/

#CanLit at the Crossroads

"7 Ways Winning a CBC Literary Prize Will Change Your Life." *CBC Books*, 12 Apr 2018. www.cbc.ca/
books/literaryprizes/7-ways-winning-a-cbc-literary-prize-will-change-your-life-1.4108650

Anderson, Benedict. *Imagined Communities: Reflections on the Origin and Spread of Nationalism.* London: Verso, 1983.

Andrusieczko, Tanya. "Statement on Joseph Boyden's Role as Contest Judge." *Briarpatch Magazine*, 18 Nov 2016. briarpatchmagazine.com/announcements/view/joseph-boydens-role-as-contest-judge

Fitzpatrick, Ryan (@ryanfitzpublic). "Nope. What gets called CanLit is historically a site of struggle." 24 Nov 2016. Tweet. twitter.com/ryanfitzpublic/status/801823282718646272

Healey, Emma. "Stories Like Passwords." *Hairpin*, 6 Oct 2014. www.thehairpin.com/2014/10/stories-like-passwords/

Lederman, Marsha. "Twitterature: Wading into the Choppy Waters of CanLit." *Globe and Mail*, 2 Feb 2018. www.theglobeandmail.com/arts/books-and-media/twitterature-wading-into-the-choppy-waters-of-canlit/article37838912/

Lewsen, Simon. "The CanLit Firestorm." *The Walrus*, 24 Nov 2016. thewalrus.ca/the-canlit-firestorm/

"Love, Anonymous." *CWILA: Canadian Women in the Literary Arts.* 2016. cwila.com/love-anonymous/

Moss, Laura. "Canada Reads." *Black Writing in Canada.* Special issue of *Canadian Literature* 182 (2004): 6–10.

Refusing the Borders of CanLit

Barrett, Paul, Darcy Ballantyne, Camille Isaacs, and Kris Singh. "The Unbearable Whiteness of CanLit." *The Walrus*, 26 July 2017. thewalrus.ca/the-unbearable-whiteness-of-canlit/

Wyile, Herb. *Anne of Tim Horton: Globalization and the Reshaping of Atlantic-Canadian Literature.* Wilfred Laurier University Press, 2011.

Hearing the Artificial Obvious

Atwood, Margaret. "Margaret Atwood on the Galloway Affair." *The Walrus*, 17 Nov 2016. thewalrus.ca/margaret-atwood-on-the-galloway-affair/

———. "Am I a Bad Feminist?" *Globe and Mail*, 13 Jan 2018. www.theglobeandmail.com/opinion/am-i-a-bad-feminist/article37591823/

Dillard, Annie. *Pilgrim at Tinker Creek.* Perennial Library, 1985.

Healey, Emma. "Stories Like Passwords." *The Hairpin*, 6 Oct 2014. www.thehairpin.com/2014/10/stories-like-passwords/

McIsaac, Julie. "And Then a Man Said It." *Wordpress.com*, 11 January 2018. andthenamansaidit.wordpress.com/

Spry, Mike. "No Names, Only Monsters: Toxic Masculinity, Concordia and Canlit." *Canlit Accountable*, 8 Jan 2018. canlitaccountable.com

Notes

Introduction

1. *Can't Lit: talking about books and stuff.* Podcast. Episode 055. cantlit.ca/
2. Bill Readings. *The University in Ruins.* Harvard University Press, 1997. 191.
3. Lauren Berlant. *Cruel Optimism.* Duke University Press, 2011.
4. Sara Ahmed. *The Cultural Politics of Emotion.* Routledge, 2013.
5. Donna J. Haraway. *Staying with the Trouble: Making Kin in the Chthulucene.* Duke University Press, 2016.
6. Warren Cariou, Heather Igloliorte, Keavy Martin, Julie Rak, Armand Ruffo, SSHRC Insight Project application, "Government Agents, Literary Agents: Inuit Books and Government Intervention, 1965–1985." March 2018. Author correspondence.
7. Kate Eichhorn and Heather Milne. *Prismatic Publics: Innovative Canadian Women's Poetry and Poetics.* Coach House Press, 2009.
8. "How Indigenous Authors Are Claiming Space in the CanLit Scene." *Unreserved.* CBC Radio. March 2018. www.cbc.ca/radio/unreserved/how-indigenous-authors-are-claiming-space-in-the -canlit-scene-1.4573996/
lee-maracle-stormed-canlit-stages-to-make-sure-her-story-was-heard-1.4578124
9. Larissa Lai, "Other Democracies: Writing Thru Race at the 20 Year Crossroad." *SmaroKamboureli* .ca January 2015. smarokamboureli.ca/wp-content/uploads/2015/01/Lai_Essay.pdf
10. Danielle Fuller and Julie Rak. "'True Stories,' Real Lives: Canada Reads 2012 and the Effects of Reading Memoir in Public." *Studies in Canada Literature* 40.2 (Winter 2016): 25–45.
11. Kathy Mezei. "A Bridge of Sorts: The Translation of Quebec Literature into English." *The Yearbook of English Studies*, Vol. 15 "Anglo-French Literary Relations" (1985): 201–26. See also Pasha Malla, "Too Different and Too Familiar: the Challenge of French-Canadian Literature." *New Yorker*, 26 May 2015. www.newyorker.com/books/page-turner/ too-different-and-too-familiar-the-challenge-of-french-canadian-literature
12. Lindsay Parnell. "Quebec Writers." Culture Trip, 9 June 2017. theculturetrip.com/north-america/ canada/quebec/articles/qu-b-cois-literature-four-great-quebec-writers/.
13. Herb Wyile and Jeannette Lynes. Introduction to "Surf's Up! The Rising Tide of Atlantic Canadian Literature" *Studies in Canadian Literature* 33.2 (2008). Also see Herb Wyile, *Anne of Tim Hortons: Globalization and the Reshaping of Atlantic-Canadian Literature*, Wilfrid Laurier University Press, 2011, and Danielle Fuller, *Writing the Everyday: Women's Textual Communities in Atlantic Canada*, McGill-Queens University Press, 2004.

14. David Hesmondhalgh. *The Cultural Industries* (second edition). Sage Publications, 2007.
15. For a case study about the monetization of celebrity within a cultural industry, see Lorraine York, *Margaret Atwood and the Labour of Literary Celebrity*. University of Toronto Press, 2013.
16. Simon Lewsen. "The CanLit Firestorm." *The Walrus*, 24 Nov 2016. thewalrus.ca/ the-canlit-firestorm/
17. Nick Mount. *Arrival: The Story of CanLit*. Anansi, 2017. 10.
18. Barbara Godard. "Notes from the Cultural Field: Canadian Literature from Identity to Hybridity," *Essays on Canadian Writing* 72 (2000): 209–247.
19. Kai Cheng Thom. "Sometimes Women Have to Make Hard Choices to Be Writers." *GUTS Magazine*, 15 Feb 2017. gutsmagazine.ca/ sometimes-women-have-to-make-hard-choices-to-be-writers/
20. The counter-letter and other resources can be accessed at sites.google.com/ualberta.ca/ counterletter/home?authuser=0
21. On June 8, 2018, the arbitrator for Galloway's appeal released his decision, finding that "certain communications" by UBC had violated Galloway's right to privacy, and awarding Galloway compensation. The decision also stated that the UBC faculty association, on Galloway's behalf, had in February 2018 withdrawn its claim for Galloway to be reinstated as a professor and receive compensation. The withdrawal of the grievance meant that the issue of whether UBC was right to fire Galloway was no longer part of the arbitration process. See Marsha Lederman, "Novelist Steven Galloway Awarded $167,000 in Damages," *Globe and Mail*, 8 June 2018. www. theglobeandmail.com/arts/books/article-novelist-steven-galloway-awarded-167000-in-damages/
22. Becky Robertson. "Authors Withdraw Their Names from Open Letter Regarding UBC's Steven Galloway Case." *Quill and Quire*, 21 Nov 2016. quillandquire.com/omni/ authors-withdraw-their-names-from-open-letter-regarding-ubcs-steven-galloway-case/
23. Jorge Barrera. "Author Joseph Boyden's Shape-shifting Indigenous Identity." *APTN News*, 23 Dec 2016. aptnnews.ca/2016/12/23/author-joseph-boydens-shape-shifting-indigenous-identity/
24. Stassa Edwards. "What Can We Learn From Canada's 'Appropriation Prize' Literary Fiasco?" *Jezebel*, 16 May 2017. jezebel.com/ what-can-we-learn-from-canadas-appropriation-prize-lite-1795175192
25. Ashifa Kassam. "Canadian Journalists Support 'Appropriation Prize' after Online Furore," *The Guardian*, 13 May 2017. www.theguardian.com/world/2017/may/13/ canadian-journalists-appropriation-prize
26. Scaachi Koul. "On Glibness and Diversity in Canadian Media." *Buzzfeed*, 12 May 2017. www.buzzfeed.com/scaachikoul/so-hows-that-whole-diversity-in-media-thing-going?utm_ term=.wqnmg9n26#.dt4p3012l
27. Maura Forrest. "All Eyez on Him: Canadian Poet Laureate Pierre DesRuisseaux Accused of Plagiarizing Tupac Shakur," *National Post*, 10 Sept 2017. nationalpost.com/news/canada/ all-eyez-on-him-canadian-poet-laureate-pierre-desruisseaux-accused-of-plagiarizing-tupac-shakur
28. See Scaachi Koul. "A Canadian Poet Who Appeared on a Shitty Media Men List Is Out of His Job." *Buzz Feed News*, 24 Jan 2018 www.buzzfeed.com/ scaachikoul/a-canadian-poet-who-appeared-on-a-shitty-media-men-list-is?utm_term=. feyMYZXM5#.exeDrBvDn. Also see Marsha Lederman, "Coach House Poetry Board Member Accused of Sexual impropriety." *The Globe and Mail*, 24 Jan 2018, updated 25 Jan 2018. www. theglobeandmail.com/arts/books-and-media/coach-house-books-board-member-accused-of-sexual-impropriety/article37727595/
29. Eithne Lynch. "Former Concordia Creative Writing Student Names Professor Who Sexually Abused Her," *the concordian*, 29 May 2018. theconcordian.com/2018/05/ former-concordia-creative-writing-student-names-professor-sexually-abused/
30. Zygmunt Bauman. *Community: Seeking Safety in an Insecure World*. Polity Press, 2001.

Part One: Refusal

1. Leanne Betasamosake Simpson and Dionne Brand. "Temporary Spaces of Joy and Freedom." *Literary Review of Canada*, June 2018. reviewcanada.ca/magazine/2018/06/temporary-spaces-of-joy-and-freedom/
2. See the introduction for a more detailed discussion of the UBCAccountable open-letter controversy.
3. Michelle Denise Smith. "Soup Cans and Love Slaves: National Politics and Cultural Authority in the Editing and Authorship of Canadian Pulp Magazines." *Book History* 9 (2006): 261–289.
4. Becky Robertson. "Authors Withdraw Their Names from Open Letter Regarding UBC's Steven Galloway Case," *Quill and Quire*, 21 Nov 2016. quillandquire.com/omni/authors-withdraw-their-names-from-open-letter-regarding-ubcs-steven-galloway-case/
5. See the introduction and note 3 to *BURN* for references to Thien's open letter.
6. William H. New. "Keith Maillard." *Encyclopedia of Literature in Canada*. University of Toronto Press, 2002. 700.
7. Zoe Whittall. "CanLit Has a Sexual-Harassment Problem," *The Walrus*, 9 Feb 2018, 30 Apr 2018. thewalrus.ca/canlit-has-a-sexual-harassment-problem/

Rape Culture, CanLit, and You

1. Peter Darbyshire, "CanLit Stars Pen Open Letter Blasting UBC over the Steven Galloway Affair," *Vancouver Sun*, 15 November 2016. vancouversun.com/news/local-news/canlit-stars-pen-open-letter-blasting-ubc-over-the-steven-galloway-affair
2. "The Criminal Justice System: Statistics." *RAINN* 2018. rain.org/statistics/criminal-justice-system
3. This tweet has been deleted.
4. Emily Lazatin (@EmilyLazatin). "Statement from @UBC..." 15 Nov 2016. 7:16 p.m. Tweet. twitter.com/EmilyLazatin/status/798726369580417024
5. Marsha Lederman (@marshalederman). "Complainant on Canlit..." 15 Nov 2016. 7:32 p.m. Tweet. twitter.com/marshalederman/status/798730406656778240
6. Marsha Lederman, "UBC Responds to Criticism over Firing of Steven Galloway," *Globe and Mail*, 15 Nov 2016. www.theglobeandmail.com/news/british-columbia/ubc-responds-to-criticism-over-firing-of-steven-galloway/article32869758/

BURN

1. Novelist and poet Keith Maillard has taught in the University of British Columbia's Creative Writing Program since 1989. Maillard wishes to point out that BC's Freedom of Information and Protection of Privacy Act forbids him from disclosing any personnel information he might have learned as a UBC employee, and he has not done so in his essay. He also wishes to emphasize that his opinions are his own and he is not speaking on behalf of the university. See the link in "Main Complainant urges university policy change" to an open letter by Joanna Birmbaum to UBC, containing quotations from a redacted version of the Boyd report. According to Birmbaum "the quotations produced above suggest Mr. Galloway engaged in sexually harassing conduct with MC before any sexual contact occurred." www.theglobeandmail.com/canada/british-columbia/article-main-galloway-complainant-urges-university-policy-change/
2. Emma Healey. "Stories Like Passwords." *The Hairpin*, 6 Oct 2014. www.thehairpin.com/2014/10/stories-like-passwords/
3. A summary of Thien's letter and a link to it are in the online version of Marsha Lederman's article "Under a Cloud." *Globe and Mail*, 28 Oct 2016. www.theglobeandmail.com/news/british-columbia/ubc-and-the-steven-galloway-affair/article32562653/ See the link in "Main Complainant urges university policy change" to an open letter by Joanna Birmbaum to UBC, containing quotations from a redacted version of the Boyd report. According to Birmbaum "the

quotations produced above suggest Mr. Galloway engaged in sexually harassing conduct with MC before any sexual contact occurred." www.theglobeandmail.com/canada/british-columbia/article-main-galloway-complainant-urges-university-policy-change/

4. Kerry Gold. "L'Affaire Galloway." *The Walrus*, 14 Sept 2016. thewalrus.ca/laffaire-galloway/

Part Two: Refuse

1. See Richard Fung, "Working through Appropriation." *Fuse* (Summer, 1993). 16–24. www.richardfung.ca/index.php?/articles/working-through-appropriation-1993/. Also see Alberto Manguel, "Letters," *Globe and Mail*, 28 March 1992.

2. Emily Riddle and Lindsay Nixon. "The Killing of Colten Boushie and Outcome of Gerald Stanley's Trial Represent a Bigger Problem," *TeenVogue*, 14 Feb 2018. www.teenvogue.com/story/the-killing-of-colten-boushie-and-outcome-of-gerald-stanleys-trial-represents-a-larger-problem

CanLit Is a Raging Dumpster Fire

1. "An Open Letter to UBC: Steven Galloway's Right to Due Process." *UBC Accountable*, 14 Nov 2016. www.ubcaccountable.com/open-letter/steven-galloway-ubc/

2. Kai Cheng Thom. "Sometimes Women Have to Make Hard Choices to be Writers." GUTS, 15 Feb 2017. gutsmagazine.ca/sometimes-women-have-to-make-hard-choices-to-be-writers/

3. Jen Sookfong Lee. "Open Letters and Closed Doors." *Humber Literary Review*. humberliteraryreview.com/jen-sookfong-lee-essay-open-letters-and-closed-doors/

4. Lenore Keeshig-Tobias. "Stop Stealing Native Stories." *Globe and Mail*, 26 Jan 1990: A7. Reprinted in *Borrowed Power: Essays on Cultural Appropriation*. Ed. Bruce Ziff and Pratima V. Rao. New Brunswick: Rutgers UP, 1997. 71–73.

5. Rinaldo Walcott. "The Unbearable Whiteness of CanLit." *The Walrus*, 26 Jul 2017. thewalrus.ca/the-unbearable-whiteness-o

6. "Jian Ghomeshi Trial: Read Highlights and Judge's Full Decision." *CBC News*, 24 Mar 2016. www.cbc.ca/news/canada/toronto/horkins-decision-ghomeshi-1.3505808

7. Robyn Doolittle. "Unfounded: Why Police Dismiss 1 in 5 Sexual Assault Claims as Baseless." *Globe and Mail*, 3 Feb 2017. www.theglobeandmail.com/news/investigations/unfounded-sexual-assault-canada-main/article33891309/

8. J. D. M. Stewart. "Don't Hold Sir John A. MacDonald to 2017's Values." *Globe and Mail*, 24 Aug 2017. www.theglobeandmail.com/opinion/dont-hold-sir-john-a-macdonald-to-2017s-values/article36083430/

Check Your Privilege!

1. Gwen Benaway. "CanLit: It's Time for the No Contact Rule." *Carte Blanche*, 12 Jun 2017. carte-blanche.org/canlit-time-no-contact-rule/

2. See Alicia Elliott, this volume.

3. James Wilt. "Canadian Media Just Created Another Alt-Right Superstar." *Canadian Dimension*, 27 Nov 2017. canadiandimension.com/articles/view/canadian-media-just-created-another-alt-right-superstar

4. Translation is my own.

5. Vivek Shraya. *even this page is white*. Vancouver: Arsenal Pulp Press, 2016. loc. 94.

6. Brit Bennett. "I Don't Know What to Do With Good White People." *Jezebel* 12 Dec 2017. jezebel.com/i-dont-know-what-to-do-with-good-white-people-1671201391

7. Joan Tronto. *Moral Boundaries: A Political Argument for an Ethic of Care*. New York: Routledge, 1993. 17–18.

8. Sumi Cho, Kimberlé Williams Crenshaw, and Leslie McCall. "Toward a Field of Intersectionality Studies: Theory, Applications, and Praxis." *Signs: Journal of Women in Culture and Society* 38.4 (2013): 785–810.

When a Cow Saves Your Life, You Learn that Audre Lorde Is Always Right

1. Dorothy Ellen Palmer. "Surrogates, Sycophants, Soldier Ants and Sheep: Debunking the Steven Galloway Innocence Project." 12 Jan 2017. dorothyellenpalmer.com/2017/01/12/surrogates -sycophants-soldier-antsand-sheep-debunking-the-steven-galloway-innocence-project/
2. Marsha Lederman. "Author Steven Galloway Makes First statement Since UBC Firing, Questions Handling of Case." *Globe and Mail*, 23 Nov 2016. www.theglobeandmail.com/news/ national/steven-galloway-ubc-firing/article33004493/
3. Marsha Lederman. "Woman Who Accused Steven Galloway of Sexual Assault Breaks Silence." *Globe and Mail*, 24 Nov 2016. www.theglobeandmail.com/news/british-columbia/woman-who -accused-author-steven-galloway-of-sexual-assault-breaks-silence/article33022923/
4. "Open Counter-Letter: Steven Galloway Case at UBC." sites.google.com/ualberta.ca/ counterletter/home?authuser=0   .
5. Carmen Aguirre. "Steven Galloway Is Innocent until Proven Guilty." *The Walrus*, 25 Nov 2016. thewalrus.ca/steven-galloway-is-innocent-until-proven-guilty/
6. Jorge Barrera. "Author Joseph Boyden's Shape-shifting Indigenous Identity." *APTN National News*, 23 Dec 2016. aptnnews.ca/2016/12/23/author-joseph-boydens-shape-shifting-indigenous-identity/. Jorge Barrera, "Similarities between Joseph Boyden Story and Ojibway Healer's Published Work Trigger Questions." *APTN National News*, 22 Feb 2017. aptnnews.ca/2017/02/22/similarities -between-joseph-boyden-story-and-ojibway-healers-published-work-trigger-questions/
7. Adoption Council of Canada. "Myths and Realities." www.adoption.ca/myths-and-realities
8. C. Baxter. "Transracial Adoption." *Canadian Paediatric Society. Paediatr Child Health*, 2006;11(7): 443–47. www.cps.ca/en/documents/position/adoption-transracial
9. "First Nations Filmmaker in Manitoba Adopting Joseph Boyden as Her Brother." *CBC News*, 13 Jan 2017. www.cbc.ca/news/indigenous/joseph-boyden-adoption-lisa-meeches-1.3935618
10. Eric Andrew-Gee. "The Making of Joseph Boyden." *Globe and Mail*, 4 Aug 2017. www. theglobeandmail.com/arts/books-and-media/joseph-boyden/article35881215/
11. C. S. Fuqua. "The Pretendian Phenomenon: Claiming Native American Ancestry." *C. S. Fuqua*, 21 Dec 2016. csfuqua.com/2016/12/21/the-pretendian-phenomenon/

CanLit Hierarchy vs. the Rhizome

1. "Our story." Rhizome Café. rhizomecafe.ca/ourstory/
2. Brampton, Ontario's Festival of Literary Diversity, or FOLD, has been around since 2016. It has a mission "to create a vibrant community of readers and writers by celebrating diverse authors and literature in Brampton, Ontario—one of Canada's most culturally diverse cities." thefoldcanada.org.
3. Feminist literary magazine *Room* "showcases writing and art by women (cisgender and transgender), transgender men, Two-Spirit and non-binary people." They hosted a feminist literary festival in Vancouver in March 2018. roommagazine.com.
4. Acerbic American model/photographer/writer Janice Dickinson has referred to herself as "the first supermodel," a disputed claim in the industry. Her modelling career was active in the seventies and eighties, and she returned to the public eye as a judge on Tyra Banks's television show *America's Next Top Model* in 2003. Following ANTM, she appeared on a series of reality shows.
5. Comedian Carrot Top (birth name Scott Thompson) is known for his bright red hair and prop comedy. Though he appears to have been working steadily since the early nineties, he's not bankable, popular, or beloved.
6. Tall poppy syndrome is an aphorism that refers to the phenomenon whereby a person who has achieved prominence among their peers must be "cut down" so they no longer stand out. The phrase is said to come from a story about Roman king Tarquin the Proud, who cut off

the heads of the tallest poppies in his garden in order to communicate that his son should kill all prominent people in a region they had occupied. It is used colloquially throughout Commonwealth countries and is similar in meaning to the Japanese aphorism "the nail that sticks out gets hammered down."

7. twitter.com/StephenMarche/status/801877240724262912
8. *Kyriarchy* is a term coined by Elisabeth Schüssler Fiorenza in 1992. It "encompasses sexism, racism, speciesism, homophobia, classism, economic injustice, colonialism, militarism, ethnocentrism, anthropocentrism, and other forms of dominating hierarchies in which the subordination of one person or group to another is internalized and institutionalized." (Wikipedia: en.wikipedia.org/wiki/Kyriarchy)
9. "Everyone's a winner." beta.theglobeandmail.com/arts/books-and-media/does-canlit -have-too-much-of-a-good-thing-when-it-comes-to-literaryprizes/article36750279/. Published Oct. 27, 2017.

How Do We Get Out of Here?

1. Ken Whyte, the founding editor of the *National Post* and editor of *Maclean's* magazine, stepped in first, offering to donate $500, and the others followed: Anne Marie Owens, editor in chief of the *National Post*; Alison Uncles, editor of *Maclean's*; Steve Maich, head of digital content and publishing at Rogers Media; Scott Feschuk, a columnist for *Maclean's*; Christie Blatchford, columnist for the *National Post*; and, shockingly, Steve Ladurantaye, the managing editor of CBC News, Canadian Broadcasting Corporation: our national broadcaster.
2. I thank editor Julie Rak for encouraging me to think about the implications of my language of academic and readerly investments in Atwood's career.

Part Three Re/Fuse

1. "Introduction: Shifting the Ground of a Discipline: Emergence and Canadian Literary Studies in English," Smaro Kamboureli and Robert Zacharias, eds., *Shifting the Ground of Canadian Literary Studies*. Wilfrid Laurier University Press, 2012. 9–10.
2. Lauren Berlant. *Cruel Optimism*. Durham: Duke University Press, 2011. 52–53.
3. Sara Ahmed. "Feminist Killjoys (And Other Willful Subjects)." *S&F Online* 8.3 (2010). 5 Dec. 2016.
4. Zoe Whittall. "CanLit Has a Sexual-Harassment Problem," *The Walrus*, 9 Feb 2018. thewalrus.ca/ canlit-has-a-sexual-harassment-problem/
5. Daniel Heath Justice. *Why Indigenous Literatures Matter*, Waterloo: Wilfrid Laurier University Press, 2018, xxi.

On Not Refusing CanLit

1. I am grateful to this student, who chooses to remain anonymous, for allowing me to share her story here. Upon granting me permission to use her words in this context, she wrote, "And if someone ever complained about why we have a required credit for Can Lit, I would like to hand them this article because I think it tells why. It is not because it's a credit you need but because there is necessity in knowing these stories and perspectives."

In the "New CanLit," We Must All Be Antigones

1. Marsha Lederman. "Twitterature: Wading into the Choppy Waters of CanLit." *Globe and Mail*, 2 Feb 2018. Web. 26 Apr 2018.
2. Chelene Knight. "Whose Story Is It? In Conversation with Alicia Elliott." *Room* magazine. Web. 26 Apr 2018.
3. CBC Books. "Jeanne Beker and Julie Black on the Nature of Healing." *CBC Books*, 29 Mar 2018. Web. 26 Apr 2018.

4. Jen SookFong Lee. "On Margaret Atwood and the New CanLit." *Open Book*. 15 Jan 2018. Web. 26 Apr 2018.

5. Alicia Elliott. "CanLit Is a Raging Dumpster Fire." *Open Book*, 7 Sep 2017. Web. 26 Apr 2018.

6. Laura Moss and Brendan McCormack. "Meanwhile, Home: Tinder Dry Conditions. *Canadian Literature*, Spring 2017. Web. 26 Apr 2018.

7. "Program Update to gritLIT." *gritLIT*. 7 Mar 2018. www.gritlit.ca/blog/program-update-to-gritlit-2018/

8. FOLD, The (TheFOLD_). "A from @jaelrichardson: "Hope is a tricky thing. For me personally, there has to be hope to keep me going. But the...t.co/OWynlhjXcb." 14 Apr 2018, 15:42 UTC. Tweet.

9. FOLD, The (TheFOLD_). "'Until I see actual systemic change, I don't have hope for the future. We aren't acknowledging what's happening in...t.co/db7dByneeK." 14 Apr 2018, 15:46 UTC. Tweet.

10. Amanda Leduc (AmandaLeduc). "I want to say something about the events that transpired yesterday at gritLit. I wanted to give space to those who...t.co/NHTioTMiTw." 15 Apr 2018, 15:24 UTC. Tweet.

11. Natalie Wee (natweewriter). "We are LITERALLY stripped of time and energy to do what we came to do because we keep explaining appropriation, hi...t.co/Y5cVGZbMDb." 14 Apr 2018, 20:50 UTC. Tweet.

12. Susan Swan (swanscribe). "I'm sorry you feel that way but I was trying to build bridges & negotiation involves compromise. It's not about one...t.co/oUzYyGje48". 02 Apr 2018, 15:50 UTC. Tweet.

13. Setoodeh Ramin. "Margaret Atwood Works to End Workplace Sexual Violence With AfterMeToo." *Variety*, 10 Apr 2018. variety.com/2018/tv/news/margaret-atwood-aftermetoo-workplace-sexual-violence-1202748002/

14. Moss and McCormack.

15. CBC Radio. "#SettlerCollector: Hashtag Helps Redirect Racist Attacks on Social Media." *Unreserved*. CBC, 18 Feb 2018. 26 Apr 2018.

16. FOLD, The (TheFOLD_). "@kayee13: 'I would like to shift us from hope to justice.'" 14 Apr 2018, 16:00 UTC. Tweet.

17. Mia Mingus. "Changing the Framework: Disability Justice." *Leaving Evidence*. 12 Feb 2011. Web. 26 Apr 2018.

Whose CanLit

1. Rosanna Deerchild. "Lee Maracle stormed CanLit stages to make sure her story was heard." *Unreserved*. CBC Radio 14 June 2018. www.cbc.ca/radio/unreserved/how-indigenous-authors-are-claiming-space-in-the-canlit-scene-1.4573996/lee-maracle-stormed-canlit-stages-to-make-sure-her-story-was-heard-1.4578124

Hearing the Artificial Obvious

1. Healey confirmed this surprise in a Twitter essay she wrote on May 22, 2018. Emma Healey (emmafromtoronto): "He DID quote my essay at length, and used other stories about me and the professor without ever using my name or linking to my piece. He used many other people's stories to make his points as well. I don't know if he had their permission. Somehow I doubt it." 22 May 2018, 1:16 p.m. Tweet. Emma Healey (emmafromtoronto): "Another fun thing was that Spry didn't think to give me (or, as far as I know, any of the women he writes about) any kind of heads-up before he published it. And of course—because he was a man, or because this stuff was suddenly newsworthy, or both—his story blew up." 22 May 2018, 1:18 p.m. Tweet.

Writing as a Rupture

1 I think of Boyden, Trudeau, and several others, writers and institutions, who have published and/or allowed appropriative texts within this last year; hell, I think of Calgary in all of its decadent Indigenous reanimations: Deerfoot, Crowchild. Blackfoot, Shaganappi. That's how my first book, *full-metal indigiqueer* was borne by playing this game I call "find the hidden NDN". There are Indigenous characters, concepts, epistemologies, languages, terminologies, etc. in everything from *Grindr* tribes to war machines—reanimation is a type of excavation, a necromancy, a necropolitic, a wildly necromantic philia. Even conceptualizations of futurisms and posthumans are inherently dependent upon a romanticized notion of posthuman (re: Indigeneity in all of its anthropologic mysticisms). A returning to pre-capitalism is a turn towards Indigenous ways of being in the holocene—at least *your* stories about them.

2 I've seen you ask for "realism" in Cherie Dimaline's *The Marrow Thieves* and Eden Robinson's *Son of a* Trickster—but hell, when the realism comes that terrifies the hell out of you— "innocence" and "realism" is a privilege you've worked out since John Locke coined the term "tabula rasa". And I've seen your ideas around Indigenous realisms—2SQ (Two-Spirit, queer Indigenous) folx as being mystics or Indigenous peoples dressed in tanned hides and furs—as if we could afford those anymore (and ain't that Ellen DeGeneres still speaking poorly of Inuk traditional foods?).

3 mistahi sêhkisiwin (we even have to put an intensifier in there, mistahi meaning much, big, to spell out horror) when it revolves around moniyawak's maci-manitôw.

Manufactured as the first edition of *Refuse: CanLit in Ruins*
in the fall of 2018 by Book*hug Press

Distributed in Canada by the Literary Press Group
lpg.ca

Distributed in the US by Small Press Distribution
Spdbooks.org

Shop online at
bookthug.ca

BOOK
PRODUCTION
WAR ECONOMY
STANDARD

Type + design by Ingrid Paulson
Copy-edited by Stuart Ross